Praise for *Worthy and Wealthy*

Emma's writing has made for an exceptional and easy read. There are eight billion people in this world and every one would get something from this book. It has a perfect balance of real-life examples, problem solving and anecdotes, but most importantly it's a very considered read, it's real, and it's very, very human.

JOEL CAINE, host, commentator, TV presenter, sports and radio broadcaster, brand ambassador

Worthy and Wealthy is the kind of book that speaks to you on a personal level. Emma Lagerlow shares her insights with such warmth and honesty, making complex ideas about wealth and self-worth feel completely relatable. It's like having a heart-to-heart with a friend who's been through it all and come out stronger. This book is a great read for anyone looking to feel more empowered in both life and finances.

LAETITIA ANDRAC, business doula, Essential Shift

'What do you want, and how will you get it?' is a question that many of us take years to answer. Emma has written a deeply personal and relatable book with both wisdom (as the name suggests), but also warmth to help you cut that journey in half. You will find immense reassurance and value in her words and work. Enjoy—and apply the practice!

KELLY IRVING, book coach, editor and founder of Expert Author Community

Highly recommended! In *Worthy and Wealthy*, Emma takes her reader on an insightful journey of self-discovery and self-determination. The book is based on Emma's own life experience and on her observation of the many clients whom Emma, as a professional Wealth and Mindset Coach, has helped to find fulfilment in their lives. Emma's compassionate approach and relaxed writing style will resonate with anyone who is struggling to make sense of their life and achieve a sense of harmony and balance.

Worthy and Wealthy is a practical, no-nonsense guide to finding true wealth and fulfilment in life. Each chapter inspires plenty of 'aha!' moments and includes a set of exercises and journal prompts that guide the reader through their own journey, gaining valuable insights along the way. If you're stuck in a life, or a lifestyle, that's not working for you, or if you often find yourself asking, 'Is this it? Surely there must be more to my life than this,' then this book is for you.

BERNARD KATES, transformational leadership coach and mentor

A book that provides a simple yet powerful framework for anyone seeking advice on how to achieve more fulfilment in life. Congratulations, Emma!

CASSANDRA LISTER, former global banker and mother of twins living a fulfilled life

I really enjoyed the 'Ikigai' concept. This is a great tool for the reader to use to ensure they don't look too far away for fulfilment in their transformation. Simply explaining how small things can have a huge impact on one's self-worth and happiness.

I've really enjoyed what I've read, there is a good blend of life examples through Jules' journey and how to use the tools to change how one sees themselves.

ROB NICHOLLS, director, AJ Grant

Emma takes us on a powerful journey in this practical and supportive guide that provides both inspiration and action to explore wealth in the broadest sense. As women, there is much complexity within our personal and professional lives and through her conversational style and colourful characters, Emma's book provides a compelling read on this important topic.

REBECCA CATTRAN, leadership and executive coach

Emma Lagerlow takes us on a journey of self-discovery and transformation through the eyes of Jules, a mother of three teetering on the brink of breakdown. Emma taps into ancient wisdom and modern psychology to help plot a course of growth through middle age, parenting and life's challenges. *Worthy and Wealthy* combines Jules' journey, Emma's real-life experiences and clear action steps to guide us through our own transformation to self-worth and true wealth.

DARREN URQUHART, founder of Rise Local

Emma truly encapsulates the importance of nourishment... feeding your body, mind and soul is imperative but enjoying the journey is just as essential.

KARA PIERCE BSC (NUT), MND accredited practising dietitian

I thoroughly enjoyed reading Emma Lagerlow's book *Worthy and Wealthy*. It is a down-to-earth guide on exploring how to develop one's happiness and wellbeing, developing a mind-set, and creating your own personal growth and wealth both spiritually and physically. The case studies made the book very relatable to anyone who is seeking change in their lives. A foolproof format that you could easily refer back to over the years.

MARTINE NICHOLLS

Worthy and Wealthy is the perfect guide to exactly what the title says… feeling more worthy and wealthy. It is the perfect blend of practical and inspiring. I feel this will be a book, no matter where you are on your journey, that you should come back to for reflection and re-evaluation. Emma connects with her audience on a deep level, connecting to where they are at in each chapter and giving support to work through to the next phase. I love the stories and the exercises. Emma really has shared her wealth of knowledge in this book and if you want support from someone who gets it, this is the perfect place to start.

MARIAH MACINNES, founder of Content Queen

Reading *Worthy and Wealthy* was truly a game changer for me. The book beautifully emphasises that transformation doesn't require giant leaps, it's all about taking tiny steps. This resonated with me deeply; it reminded me that only I can change my life and that the power to shape my future lies within my hands. The encouragement to embrace my potential and be whoever I choose has inspired me to step outside my comfort zone and continue evolving as a person. I love how each chapter feels like a fresh start, a new opportunity to rewrite my story. This book opened my eyes to the fact that transforming my life into what I want it to be is not only possible but entirely within my reach. If you're ready to ignite your own light bulb moment, I wholeheartedly recommend this book. It's a must read for anyone looking to embrace change and live authentically!

LISA BRANCH

Worthy and Wealthy is a transformative read for women who sense, deep in their souls, that greater happiness and fulfilment are within reach but are unsure how to attain them. This insightful life guide masterfully navigates the various facets of life, encouraging you to reflect and integrate the changes your true self needs and desires for a more connected, authentic, and deeply satisfying existence.

LISA HODGSON, declutter and minimalism coach

I loved reading *Worthy and Wealthy*; Emma really makes you think about what you want out of life. It's a book I will read over and over again. Five stars from me!

LEANNE CAFE, Pilates instructor

This book is an empowering resource for anyone looking to take control of their life. From the first page it captivated me with its relatable stories and practical tools, making it an absolute page turner. It's written in a way that's easy to read, yet it offers profound insights into creating a more meaningful and purposeful life. As I read, I found myself unravelling the complexities of my own busy life and gaining clarity on my goals and direction. This is a book you'll want to revisit time and time again as it helps you reassess your goals and guides you towards lifetime fulfilment.

NADINE BISHOP, primary educator

I am honoured to recommend *Worthy and Wealthy* by Emma Lagerlow, a transformative, inspiring and empowering exploration into self-acceptance and the true meaning of wealth. Emma presents readers with the tools to redefine their relationship with wealth and self-worth, blending personal experiences with practical advice and tools to guide and remind us that it's never too early or too late to take this personal journey. Emma's authentic voice and genuine passion for helping others shines through, making readers feel as if they're having a heartfelt conversation with a trusted friend. Thank you, Emma, for sharing your wisdom and encouraging us all to embrace our worthiness!

TRACY THEW, manager, Australian Golf Club Ski Lodge, Perisher Valley

Emma has a unique way of extracting the best from her readers by encouraging them to delve into their thoughts on self-worth, beliefs and purpose. Through clearly laid out processes with actionable tasks and journal prompts, the audience has the tools and guidance to become their best selves. I highly recommend this book!

AVRIL LILLIAN, graphic designer and business owner

This book radiates warmth, guidance and heartfelt wisdom. From start to finish, it feels like a gentle conversation with a close confidant, inviting you to pause, reflect and grow. The author's beautifully woven metaphors of a butterfly's transformation, paired with thoughtful prompts and rich storytelling, create a space for self-discovery that is both natural and deeply nurturing. It's a journey paved with hope, reflection and care—perfect for anyone seeking a supportive guide on their personal journey.

LEA RAUSCH, startup operator, consultant, writer and speaker

WORTHY
&
WEALTHY

WORTHY & WEALTHY

Discovering Abundance and Fulfilment Beyond Money

Emma Lagerlow

GRAMMAR
FACTORY
— EST? 2013 —

Grammar Factory Publishing
MacMillan Company Limited
25 Telegram Mews, 39th Floor, Suite 3906
Toronto, Ontario, Canada
M5V 3Z1

www.grammarfactory.com

Lagerlow, Emma.
Worthy and Wealthy: Discovering Abundance and Fulfilment Beyond
Money / Emma Lagerlow.

Paperback ISBN 978-1-998528-02-8
Hardcover ISBN 978-1-998528-04-2
eBook ISBN 978-1-998528-03-5
Audiobook ISBN 978-1-998528-14-1

1. BUS050000 BUSINESS & ECONOMICS / Personal Finance / General.
2. BUS107000 BUSINESS & ECONOMICS / Personal Success.
3. SEL023000 SELF-HELP / Personal Growth / Self-Esteem.

PRODUCTION CREDITS
Cover design by Designerbility
Interior layout design by Setareh Ashrafologhalai
Book production and editorial services by Grammar Factory Publishing

GRAMMAR FACTORY'S CARBON NEUTRAL PUBLISHING COMMITMENT
Grammar Factory Publishing is proud to be neutralising the carbon foot-
print of all printed copies of its authors' books printed by or ordered
directly through Grammar Factory or its affiliated companies through the
purchase of Gold Standard-Certified International Offsets.

To Aaron, a.k.a. Chugga, my rock and forever companion. You've stood by my side through every crazy idea, leap of faith and reinvention of myself. I've been laughing and loving the whole way, and your unwavering support has given me the wings to soar.

To Ben, Ella, Zoe and Sarah—my heart and ultimate inspiration. Thank you for your grace and patience. My greatest accomplishment will always be being your mum.

And to you, my dear readers—this book is for you. May it serve as a guiding light on your journey towards a life filled with abundance and fulfilment. Always remember, you are worthy of all the wealth, love and joy this world has to offer.

CONTENTS

INTRODUCTION

CATERPILLAR

There's a part of every living thing
that wants to become itself:
the tadpole into the frog, the chrysalis
into the butterfly, a damaged
person into a whole one.

ELLEN BASS
American author and poet

JULES' MOBILE PHONE alarm cuts through her light snoring, waking her with a start; it's 5 am. Her head is pounding, and she calculates despairingly that she's gotten around six hours of sleep. She quickly decides that there's no wine allowed tonight.

Jules grabs her keys, shuffles out into the dark and cold morning and hops into her SUV. It still has a new smell, which brings a rush of pleasure. That feeling is not long-lived, as Jules immediately recalls the repayments she can't afford. After separating from Dean, buying the car seemed like a good idea—something to mark the new chapter.

Jules yawns and her eyes water all the way to the park, where she meets some friends and other women for training. She attends She Fit three times a week at 5:30 am.

She arrives home without noticing her route because she's so caught up in the mental checklist of everything she needs to do before work and school drop-off. The mental checklist helps to quell Jules' underlying anxiety. Being busy is a coping mechanism that soothes her misaligned soul.

Jules wakes the kids and asks what they each want for breakfast. She starts the washing machine and is reminded that it needs a service when it whines. She resentfully adds this to her mental list.

Chloe and Jimmy are surly when they enter the kitchen, and Mia skips around playfully as usual, which annoys the older tweens. Mia, in her excitement, knocks over a glass of juice, and Jules loses her shit. A primordial scream escapes her lips. The room goes silent, and everyone thinks the same thing.

Is Mum going to lose it?

Jules somehow manages to contain her frustration, but you can cut the air with a knife, and Mia starts whimpering. Jules feels her fear. 'Sorry, mummy,' Mia says. Jules doesn't say a word back. All the kids are walking on eggshells, and Jules wishes she could stem the burning anger and resentment bubbling within, but she has just enough energy to stop letting out another blood-curdling scream.

She's going to be late.

Driving through the back streets of the leafy suburbia on her way to work, Jules wonders what her life is all about. All she yearned for growing up was a family of her own, and now she has one, but she also has an emotionally abusive ex-partner, and her kids are not what she imagined. Most days, they act entitled and spoiled. Jules drops the kids off, still nursing a hangover from too much wine the night before. She's barely aware of the kids getting out of the car because she's so worried about the measly $1,200 in her bank account, which must last for the next week and pay the rent due in two days.

The mental load feels unbearable.

Jules gets to work five minutes late, with all eyes on her as she walks in. She gets to her desk and switches on her computer.

Sitting there, Jules daydreams about winning Powerball, even though she doesn't have a ticket. She imagines telling her boss where he can stick his job and giving everyone the bird as she walks out the door, preferably with a one-way ticket to Hawaii.

Jules is brought back to reality with a start when her boss asks if she has any ideas for the upcoming Christmas party.

Somehow, Jules makes it through the day. She buys mince at lunchtime to make spaghetti for dinner, which she cooks between dropping the kids off at their classes and then picking them up again, along with a bottle of wine.

Jules finishes cleaning the kitchen after dinner. She polishes off her second glass of wine, pours a third, folds a mountain of washing and watches *Emily in Paris* on Netflix. Absentmindedly, Jules wishes she was thirty-something again, living in Paris with the world at her feet.

Jules eventually falls asleep after taking a sleeping tablet at 12:45 am. She's spent, exhausted, resentful, and dreading the same kind of day tomorrow. Her last thought before sleep finds her: *how did life get to this point?*

I WROTE THIS book because you may feel dissatisfied with yourself and your life, just like I once did.

I write a lot about Jules, a fictional character I resonate with deeply. I believe you might resonate with her, too.

Jules is at a low ebb and living her life on autopilot. She is yearning for more harmony, meaningful connection and wealth, but is grappling with unhealthy habits, compulsive spending, strained relationships and financial struggles.

Jules' deeper issues lie in self-awareness, self-worth and self-belief. She lacks healthy boundaries and an overall sense of purpose, but has no idea how to get from where she is to the worthy and wealthy life that she imagines for herself.

Allow Jules to be your friend and guide as you read, experiencing the transformative journey with you, hand in hand.

Please also allow me to guide you as you flutter through these pages. I'm Emma Lagerlow, and a few years ago, I could see myself in Jules in more ways than one. I was 100% living on autopilot and resentful and dissatisfied with my life in many ways. Don't get me wrong, I have a very privileged life, and I was grateful to have a twenty-five-year corporate career that held me in good stead to create a wonderful life for myself and my family. I had a great partner, great friendships and created many meaningful memories in my forty-five years on Earth.

But when the Covid-19 pandemic appeared out of the blue and completely turned everyone's lives upside down in March 2020, it awakened me. Little did I know I was simultaneously navigating early menopause while raising teenagers, some of whom were facing neurodiverse challenges and other health issues. In hindsight, these were all catalysts for me to transform my life.

I took a leap of faith and resigned from my marketing role at the end of 2021; the rest is history. I now host in-person meditation and sound healing events, and have a podcast called *It's a Mindset*, group coaching programs and a thriving coaching practice.

I've since integrated more wellbeing into my life and discovered my purpose through holistic wealth and mindset coaching. Everyone can find true worth and wealth and live an unimaginably fulfilling life—a life where you feel well in both body and mind, nurture meaningful connections, embrace enriching experiences, and understand that money is simply a tool for achieving your purpose, and granting you greater autonomy and freedom over your time.

While it has, without a doubt, been a roller coaster ride, I have learned so much about myself and now find deep fulfilment in my work. Everything I preach in my coaching, I have lived through myself. So, you can trust me when I say—I've been where you are.

This book's five chapters focus on key themes essential to transforming your life that I have found to be trusted and true both in my life and the lives of my clients: worthiness, purpose, wellbeing, wealth and freedom. Each chapter is filled with insights, exercises, research and case studies I've used in my life and with clients I've worked with as a holistic wealth and mindset coach. You will realise that it's not just financial wealth and material possessions but the intangible, internal parts of yourself that make you who you are and are essential to changing your life.

I've used the life cycle of a butterfly as an analogy to illustrate this journey. A butterfly starts out as a caterpillar, sluggishly moving through life to ultimately find true wealth and fulfilment, like a beautiful butterfly embarking on a new beginning.

So, what are the five transformative pillars, and how do you create a worthy, wealthy life full of abundance?

The 5 Worthy and Wealthy Pillars

Chapter 1: Chrysalis
In this chapter, we explore who you are by uncovering and gaining awareness of your core beliefs, allowing you to better understand your authentic self, identify where your life may be out of harmony, and enhance your self-worth.

Chapter 2: Metamorphosis
What do you want, and how will you get it? We will explore this in Chapter 2, which is all about finding your purpose and determining your core values. Visualisation and affirmations

are both explored in this chapter. These tools and others will help you nurture your mental health and get you thinking about your path towards a deeply worthy and wealthy life.

Chapter 3: Nectar
Once you have a strong sense of self, you'll find prioritising your health easier. We'll explore wellbeing in this chapter and focus on self-care practices such as meditation, journaling, and other health-building habits that serve as your nectar, helping to align your body, mind and soul to achieve all you desire.

Chapter 4: Wings
By the time you reach Chapter 4, you'll have a clear sense of who you are and what you truly desire. This pillar centres on achieving financial stability and transforming your relationship with money. Your personal wealth acts as the wind beneath your wings, empowering you to soar towards financial success.

Chapter 5: Fly
In this closing chapter, we'll delve into goal setting and the power of manifestation to help you reach the heights of abundance and fulfilment that you envision. Financial freedom is the conduit to time autonomy, allowing you true freedom to fill your life with meaning and joy.

As you read this, I understand you may be wallowing in dissatisfaction, resentment, fear or hopelessness about your life. Or perhaps you're simply intrigued and searching for more clarity, fulfilment or purpose.

You're not alone in these feelings and don't have to continue this path. When you know who you are, what you want, and how to get it, you will achieve greater worth and wealth than you ever imagined possible.

Are you ready to embark on this transformative journey? Let's do this.

1

CHRYSALIS

I AM WORTHY

Knowing yourself is the
beginning of all wisdom.

ARISTOTLE

THE MOMENT that Jules asked herself the burning question—*How did life get to this point?*—was the moment that things began to change. She booked a wellness retreat on a whim, but it was more than an impulse buy. It was the catalyst of positivity that she needed to commit to changing her life. The retreat organiser, Penny, suggested that Jules contact a life coach named Amanda. Over several months, Amanda gently brought Jules back to her authentic self.

Together, they worked through exercises to see where Jules' life was out of balance. Not much of her life was in harmony, and Jules wondered how she was not completely burned out. Her three kids likely kept her head above water, but barely.

When Jules began exploring her beliefs with Amanda, her limiting beliefs also came to the fore. She realised how much trauma, hurt and rejection she had been holding onto from her late teens when she felt unloved and disowned by her parents. This rejection profoundly impacted her self-worth and she developed people-pleasing tendencies to satisfy her deep need for belonging.

As a result of these experiences, Jules formed a subconscious belief early in life that she was never good enough for the people she loved.

These unresolved life experiences were likely why Jules fell into negative patterns, allowing other people to belittle her emotionally, including her ex-husband. It was what she believed she deserved.

There were some dark times as Jules was forced to face the actual reality of her situation, but there was also empowerment.

Once Jules shifted her mindset, everything began to fall into place. She could see clearly that she was undervalued at work and not earning what she deserved. No longer willing to settle for less, Jules took control of her career and began searching for a new role where her value was recognised and appreciated.

KNOWING WHO YOU truly are and understanding what is holding you back is the key to creating a life of fulfilment, success and wealth—both emotionally and materially. This chapter lays the foundation for that transformation by diving into your conscious and subconscious beliefs, with the aim of healing and rebuilding your self-esteem and confidence. Through a combination of exploratory exercises and aligned mindset-shifting affirmations, you'll begin the powerful journey of connecting with the most authentic version of yourself.

At the heart of this work lies the concept of self-worth—an intrinsic belief that you are valuable, deserving of happiness, and worthy of success and respect simply because of who you are. Unlike self-esteem, which can fluctuate based on external validation, self-worth is rooted in an unwavering sense of inner value. Cultivating self-worth is essential, as it shapes how you perceive your capabilities, approach challenges and pursue your goals. If your self-worth is low, it's often because limiting beliefs—those hidden, self-sabotaging thoughts—are standing in the way of realising your true potential.

As we delve deeper into your core and limiting beliefs, you'll begin to recognise and challenge thoughts that no longer serve you. This awareness empowers you to make new choices and embrace meaningful change. After all, you cannot change what you are not aware of. Only by bringing these beliefs to light can you transform them. Like a caterpillar shedding its old form to become a butterfly, this transformation will help you reclaim your true self and live a life that reflects your most authentic, worthy and wealthy self.

You will learn about the Wheel of Life exercise to identify where your life may be out of harmony. You will also explore your core beliefs, including limiting beliefs, through helpful exercises. Finally, you will create positive affirmations to guide your inner healing and rewire your limiting beliefs. These crucial exercises and practices will help solidify your foundational sense of worthiness, allowing you to spread your wings in future chapters. Let's start with your Wheel of Life.

Wheel of Life

The Wheel of Life exercise is an excellent tool to help you see where your life may be out of harmony. This exercise involves evaluating key areas of your life and identifying where you might need to focus more attention.

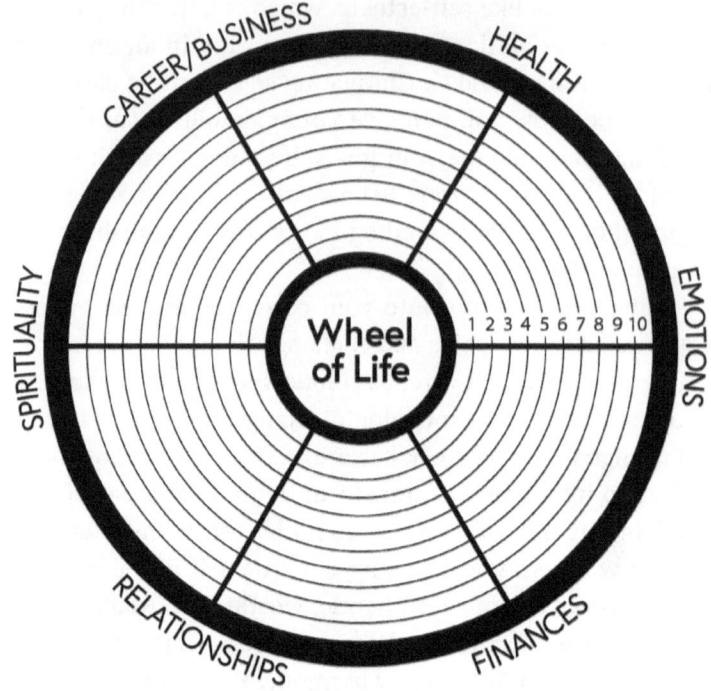

FIGURE 1 Wheel of Life

To complete the Wheel of Life exercise, follow these steps:

Step 1—Recreate the Wheel
Draw a circle and divide it into six pieces, as shown in Figure
1. Alternatively, you can use the one provided in this book.
Label each section with the following areas: Health, Emotions,
Finances, Relationships, Spirituality and Career/Business.

Step 2—Rate Each Area
Rate each area on a scale of one to ten, with one being the
lowest and ten being the highest. This rating is based on

your perception; there are no right or wrong answers. Place a dot on each line at the point representing your rating for that area. For example, if you rate your health as a six out of ten, place a dot at six on the health line.

Step 3—Reflect and Journal

After rating each area, consider times when you might have rated that area higher. Write about what has changed since that time. For instance, consider factors like nutrition or exercise routine changes if your health rating has dropped. Journal your thoughts to gain deeper insights. For the different sections, consider the following:

Health

- What has impacted your health rating?

- Are there habits you need to reintroduce, such as meal prepping or regular exercise?

Emotions

- Reflect on your emotional wellbeing.

- Would practices like meditation help improve this area?

Finances

- Consider setting up a budget to help you feel more confident, in control and empowered.

Relationships

- Consider ways to enhance your relationships. This could include marriage counselling, joining social groups, or finding new ways to connect with loved ones such as planning date nights, organising special outings with your children or catching up with friends.

Spirituality

* Reflect on your spiritual practices. This can be religious or spiritual activities, including mindfulness, nature walks, or other activities that nourish your soul.

Career/Business

* Assess your satisfaction with your career or business.

* Are there steps you can take to improve this area, such as seeking further education or making a career change?

Step 4—Identify Actions

In a journal, write down points about what you can do to improve each area. This will give you a comprehensive view of your life and highlight areas needing more attention. To start, aim for one action for each area of your life.

By completing this exercise, you'll gain self-awareness and identify specific actions you can take to create more balance and harmony. Self-awareness is everything, and this exercise can be a powerful step towards a truly wealthy and fulfilling life.

CLIENT STORY

Heather, a client in her early forties, came to me seeking extra support. After enduring a painful divorce and delays in selling her family home, she moved back in with her parents and teenage daughter. She felt lost and despondent during our Zoom coaching calls, which she attended from her childhood bedroom.

Through the Wheel of Life coaching exercises outlined in this chapter, we uncovered that Heather had been neglecting healthy eating and physical activity since moving in with her parents. With all her belongings in storage, prioritising her fundamental wellbeing became challenging. Her busy schedule, juggling a part-time job as a business administrator and a side hustle as a virtual assistant (VA), further constrained her time, making it difficult to achieve optimal wellbeing.

Given her circumstances, we set up some achievable accountability measures for Heather's wellbeing. After uncovering her core values—achievement, truth, stability and relationships—and challenging her limiting beliefs around not knowing enough and having imposter syndrome, Heather began to see her purpose as an excellent creator and business organiser. She was ready to start life on her terms.

In the later coaching sessions, we worked on uncovering Heather's purpose, which centred around using her organisational skills and creative talents to help businesses thrive in the digital landscape and give her greater time freedom. She set clear goals, and within three months of working together, Heather had accomplished a great deal. She purchased and moved into her dream home, went on an overseas holiday with her daughter and partner, resigned from her part-time job and committed fully to her VA business. Heather was set on the path to achieving everything she wanted out of life.

How did she do it?

Once Heather moved and settled into her new home, she joined a gym close to where she lived and began to work out consistently, improving her health rating on the Wheel of Life. With her belongings out of storage, she was able to stock up on healthy food and resumed meal prepping, which not only boosted her physical health but also elevated her emotional wellbeing.

As Heather addressed the areas of imbalance in her life, she also turned her attention to the deeper work of challenging her imposter syndrome. This limiting belief had held her back by making her feel inadequate, as though she didn't know enough to succeed. However, through identifying this belief and reframing it, Heather's confidence grew. Feeling more aligned with her true self, she took the leap to resign from corporate life and fully committed to her VA business, increasing her career satisfaction. This newfound autonomy allowed Heather to work from anywhere, deepening her relationships with her daughter and partner through quality time and further enhancing her overall sense of fulfilment.

By addressing both the surface imbalances through the Wheel of Life and the deeper internal beliefs that had been holding her back, Heather achieved a powerful transformation. This balance not only created harmony in her life but also allowed her to unlock a more fulfilled and free existence.

Your Core Beliefs

An important part of growing your self-worth is uncovering your core beliefs. Core beliefs are deep-seated thoughts and assumptions about yourself, others, and the world around you. These beliefs can be both positive and negative. For instance, a negative belief like 'Everyone else is better at their job than I am' often arises from comparing yourself to others, leading to feelings of inadequacy and imposter syndrome. This limiting belief can erode your confidence, even in the face of your accomplishments. These beliefs often remain unnoticed in the subconscious, yet powerfully shape your life.

Negative core beliefs can significantly impact what you achieve and how you behave. If you hold inaccurate or negative beliefs about yourself, they can drastically reduce your chances of experiencing joy and fulfilment. Some common negative core beliefs include 'I'm not good enough,' 'There's not enough money to go around,' or 'Money is the root of all evil.'

Believing 'I'm not good enough' might stop you from applying for jobs or promotions. Holding the belief 'There's not enough money to go around' can lead to frugal behaviours that limit your experience of abundance. Similarly, believing 'Money is the root of all evil' might cause you to subconsciously reject financial wealth, fearing that others will think less of you or dislike you for being financially successful.

Awareness of your core beliefs is key to unpacking and transforming them. These beliefs are often formed in the imprint stage of life, from birth to seven years old, when we absorb ideas and values from our parents, caregivers and significant life events. These beliefs, deeply embedded in your subconscious, frequently go unquestioned. When unsupportive, they evolve into limiting patterns that dictate your behaviour and hold you back from living your best life.

Limiting beliefs can arise from significant traumas like accidents, illnesses or deaths. However, they can also form from smaller traumas. For instance, when a teacher at school told you that you were drawing a rainbow wrong, you might have begun to hold yourself back from being creative for fear of rejection or criticism. Another common example is being bullied or rejected by peers at school, which can instil the belief that you aren't worthy of friendship or belonging. This belief can linger into adulthood, causing you to withdraw from social interactions or suppress your true self to avoid rejection.

Many limiting beliefs are formed to protect ourselves from perceived threats, similar to how we might react to the threat of an imaginary tiger. In the past, being cast out of a tribe could mean struggling to survive. Without the safety of the group, individuals faced greater risks of starvation, predation or exposure to the elements. Without the protection, food, shelter and emotional support the group provides, survival could become extremely difficult, if not impossible. Consequently, humans learned to adapt behaviours to avoid rejection or exclusion from the tribe.

Although modern life has evolved to provide more safety and security, our primitive brain has not fully caught up. It still interprets emotional or psychological triggers—like social rejection, failure or perceived inadequacy—as existential threats to belonging and survival. This often causes us to suppress or hide unique aspects of ourselves that seem different or that we perceive as threatening to our wellbeing.

Your body doesn't know the difference between a real or an imaginary tiger, reacting to triggers as if they are real, throwing you into fight, flight, fawn or freeze mode. This means your body responds to perceived threats just as it would to real ones. When this happens, your body is not operating in homeostasis. Not only does this hold you back from achieving what you want at that moment, but it also affects your body's optimal performance, allowing symptoms and illnesses to creep in past the usual hardy barriers you have in place when you're running with clarity on all cylinders.

Uncovering limiting beliefs and building self-worth are closely intertwined. When you understand that your inherent value is not dependent on external achievements or validation from others, you begin to unravel the limiting beliefs that hold you back. This foundational work is essential for creating a truly wealthy life, one that is rich in fulfilment, confidence and self-acceptance.

Some ways you can uncover your limiting beliefs include exploring healing modalities such as counselling, psychology, life coaching, kinesiology, hypnotherapy, meditation or journaling. These can all help you identify and understand the beliefs that may hinder you from creating a truly worthy and wealthy life.

Let's begin right now by setting aside thirty to forty-five minutes of quiet time for this journaling exercise. Find a comfortable place to sit with your journal or blank paper.

Step 1—Reflect on Key Areas of Your Life
Begin by thinking about different areas of your life. Write down your thoughts and feelings about each of these areas:

- Health
- Emotions
- Finances
- Relationships
- Spirituality
- Business/Career

Step 2—Identify Recurrent Thoughts

For each area, note any recurrent limiting thoughts or feelings that come up. Ask yourself:

- What thoughts do I often have about this area?

- How do I feel about this part of my life?

- Are there any specific memories or experiences that stand out?

Step 3—Recognise Patterns and Themes

Look for patterns and themes in your thoughts and feelings. Are there any common threads? Write down any beliefs or assumptions that repeatedly appear, even if they seem minor.

Step 4—Dig Deeper

- For each belief you've identified, ask yourself the following questions and journal your responses:

  - Where did this belief originate? (Consider your childhood, significant life events or influential people. Was this belief repeated often? Why did you trust the person who told you this, and is there a reason to believe the opposite?)

  - How has this belief affected my life? (Consider both positive and negative impacts.)

  - Is this belief still serving me or is it holding me back?

Step 5—Challenge and Reframe

- Choose one limiting belief to focus on and aim to reverse the experience that originally caused you to hold onto it. It doesn't matter how often you hear the opinion—it's essential to recognise that, as an adult, you can now distinguish between opinion and fact. Ask yourself these questions and journal your answers:

- Is this belief absolutely true?

- What evidence do I have that contradicts this belief?

- How would my life be different if I no longer held this belief?

- What new, empowering belief can I adopt to replace this limiting one?

Here's an example from Jules' life:

Limiting Belief: 'I'm not good enough to succeed in my career.'

Origin: Jules' limiting belief likely began in her late teenage years, rooted in feelings of rejection and misunderstanding from her parents, which negatively affected her self-worth. Over time, her relationship with Dean, her ex-husband, reinforced this belief. Dean frequently belittled her, much like his father had done to his own wife, which only deepened Jules' belief that she wasn't good enough. Despite hoping for change, Dean would briefly improve after arguments, only to revert to his critical behaviour. The final wake-up call came when Jules noticed her children beginning to mirror Dean's disdain towards her. This prompted her to take a stand, end the marriage, and prevent the toxic cycle from affecting her children. However, comparing herself to peers in supportive relationships and secure careers only compounded her feelings of inadequacy, making her believe she couldn't balance work and family, thus solidifying the belief that she wasn't good enough to succeed professionally.

Impact: This limiting belief caused Jules to avoid pursuing promotions or new challenges in her career, driven by fear of failure and rejection. As a result, she held herself back from opportunities that could have advanced her professionally. Jules' feelings of inadequacy also led to unhealthy coping mechanisms, such as compulsive spending, which further perpetuated her belief that she wasn't competent enough, even in managing her finances.

Truth Check: With the help of her life coach, Amanda, Jules began to uncover a powerful truth—she was, in fact, succeeding both personally and professionally. She was raising her children with unconditional love and guiding them to be good humans while also modelling the importance of standing up for oneself by leaving an emotionally abusive relationship. Despite the challenges, Jules had managed to balance single motherhood and her career, completing key projects at work with positive outcomes and earning praise from her manager and colleagues. This history of achievement directly contradicted her belief that she couldn't succeed in her career.

New Belief: 'I am capable and deserving of success in my career.'

Jules began to actively challenge her limiting belief by acknowledging her past successes and embracing opportunities that aligned with her strengths. By shifting her mindset, she rebuilt her confidence and empowered herself to pursue career success without fear of failure.

Step 6—Affirmation

- Create an affirmation based on your new belief and incorporate it into your daily routine. Write it on a Post-it note and place it somewhere visible, like your bathroom mirror, fridge, bedside table, phone wallpaper or screen saver, so it becomes a consistent part of your day. For example: 'I am capable and deserving of success in my career.' Speak it aloud daily with intention, feeling each word as you visualise yourself thriving professionally. This seemingly small action can gradually transform your mindset, aligning your thoughts with your future vision of yourself. It's essential to create an affirmation that resonates deeply with you. If you're not fully aligned or don't genuinely believe in the affirmation, it could unintentionally hold you back.

Through this practice, you'll begin uncovering the limiting beliefs that have held you back and begin to challenge them. As you reframe them into empowering thoughts, you'll find your perspective shifting, opening space for personal growth, fulfilment and success. This reversal of old imprints in itself is healing, and it all begins with simple awareness.

Journal Prompt—Belief Affirmation

You can use your new beliefs to form a belief affirmation that may support you as you navigate life. You may consider creating a belief affirmation that contradicts one or several of your limiting beliefs. For instance, like Jules, if your limiting beliefs have centred around feeling inadequate or believing you're incapable of success in your career, your belief affirmation could be:

'I am worthy of success in all areas of my life. My experiences have shaped me into a resilient, capable individual who is deserving of growth, happiness and fulfilment. I release my past fears and embrace new opportunities with confidence in my ability to thrive, both personally and professionally.'

This affirmation directly opposes Jules' past limiting beliefs and serves to reinforce a positive, empowering mindset. By focusing on your strengths and innate worthiness, you can use this as a daily affirmation to keep your mindset aligned with your goals.

You can even use AI tools like ChatGPT to help generate belief affirmations or craft one that resonates with you personally. Simply provide a prompt that reflects the kind of affirmation you're seeking. For example, you could prompt with: 'I want to create a belief statement that instils confidence and helps me overcome imposter syndrome.' Based on this, ChatGPT might generate something like: 'I am fully capable, and my unique talents bring value and success. I deserve every opportunity that comes my way.'

Don't hesitate to experiment with different wording until you find an affirmation that truly feels aligned. As stated previously, it's vital to fully believe in your affirmation, as any misalignment can hinder your progress rather than propel you forward.

Remember, core beliefs aren't fixed. They will shift as you grow and develop, especially as you continue to bring awareness to them and challenge limiting beliefs. Depending on your life circumstances, some beliefs may become more significant at different times. Revisit this exercise periodically to ensure your beliefs continue to serve and empower you.

NOW LET'S RETURN to Jules and her sessions with her life coach, Amanda. As they continued with the sessions, Jules began to experience moments of disbelief and anger, realising how much of her life had been shaped and limited by her insecurities. She felt a mix of frustration and sadness as she recognised how these limiting beliefs had held her back. But as she worked through these feelings, Jules began to reconnect with a sense of purpose and possibility. She remembered how much she loved helping people, and a seed began to be sown.

Armed with newfound confidence, Jules sought a role that better suited her lifestyle and allowed her to be more present for her kids. Boldly, she resigned from her job where she had long felt undervalued and found a position at a private psychology practice with school-friendly hours. This new role provided the flexibility to align her career with her children's schedules, giving her both the time and energy to be more involved in their lives. The change not only created space for her to be the mother she wanted to be, but also allowed her to pursue a more fulfilling career.

Sometime after her work with Amanda had concluded, Jules decided to make more changes in her life. She tapered off drinking during the week—a ritual that had once been a near-daily habit—and though breaking this pattern took time, it led to noticeable improvements. Jules found herself sleeping better, feeling more patient and experiencing a greater sense of calm. Even her shopping addiction, which had once served as a coping mechanism, began to fade.

By learning more about herself and challenging her limiting beliefs, Jules began to reclaim control over her life. She was no longer willing to waste precious time living in fear of being her authentic self and pursuing her dreams. Just as Jules reclaimed her life, so can you.

CHAPTER HIGHLIGHTS

- **Understanding and recognising core beliefs**: Core beliefs are the deeply ingrained assumptions we hold about ourselves, others and the world. These beliefs are often shaped during childhood or through significant life events and can be both positive and negative. Subconsciously, core beliefs influence our behaviours, choices and emotional responses in profound ways. By bringing these core beliefs into awareness, we open the door to a deeper understanding of ourselves, laying the foundation for greater self-worth, personal growth and fulfilment. This mindset shift leads to a more empowered way of living.

- **Self-reflection through the Wheel of Life**: The Wheel of Life exercise provides a powerful visual tool to assess balance across key areas of life, including Health, Emotions, Finances, Relationships, Spirituality and Career. This exercise highlights where your life might be out of balance and offers insights into where more attention is needed. With this clarity, you can take actionable steps to create more harmony in your life as you continue to grow and evolve.

- **Shifting limiting beliefs**: Becoming aware of limiting beliefs is the first step towards transforming them into empowering ones. Mindset-shifting exercises and positive affirmations can help you reshape the negative thoughts that once held you back. As you consistently reframe limiting beliefs into empowering ones, you'll cultivate confidence and develop a more resilient, optimistic outlook. This shift enhances your personal growth and unlocks new opportunities for professional success, helping you move forward with a stronger sense of self-worth and possibility.

- **Actionable steps for lasting change**: Awareness alone does not create lasting change—consistent action does. This chapter equips you with practical tools such as journaling, self-reflection and affirmations to actively challenge limiting beliefs and replace them with more empowering ones. These actionable steps support your journey of self-discovery and transformation, guiding you towards growing your self-worth and creating the life you deserve.

2

METAMORPHOSIS

I HAVE PURPOSE

The Japanese word 'ikigai' is composed of two characters: iki, which means 'life', and gai, which means 'worth'. It's usually translated as 'a reason to live', or simply, 'a reason to get up in the morning'.

IKIGAI, HÈCTOR GARCIA and
FRANCESC MIRALLES

ONCE JULES was well into the transformative phase of her life, she began deeply reconnecting with herself and discovering new layers of purpose. For years, her priority had been caring for others, often following in her mother's footsteps as the family organiser and budgeter. But by the time she reached this phase, Jules was beginning to realise there was more to her than managing household responsibilities. She felt called to explore a deeper sense of self and purpose beyond the roles she'd always known.

Through her work with Amanda, Jules learned that money certainly isn't the be-all or end-all. She came to understand that cultivating a strong sense of self and self-worth is the key to feeling content and fulfilled.

Jules spent a powerful session with Amanda, focusing on her core values. While some time was spent confronting emotions of frustration and regret, many of the emotions she felt were uplifting and pinpointed Jules' values of belonging, empathy and vitality. It was incredibly empowering. Jules began to see herself in a new light. She recalled how she loved dancing when she was younger and, with Amanda's encouragement, found an adult jazz class, which she absolutely loved.

Amanda also introduced Jules to the concept of ikigai—a reason for being—and encouraged her to meditate and journal. These practices helped Jules clarify what truly mattered to her, and brought her closer to discovering her unique purpose. Though she was starting to feel worthy of her hopes and dreams, she realised that she wasn't yet fully clear on what those dreams were. But this only excited her more, as she felt ready to uncover them step by step.

AS I REFLECT on Jules' journey, I can't help but think about my own growing fascination with the concept of ikigai. Japan, with its rich traditions and unique way of life, captivated me in my travels in ways I hadn't expected.

One memory stands out vividly: my family and I were snowboarding in Myoko, a beautiful, serene Japanese village. It was the end of the season, so the resort was relatively quiet. What struck me most wasn't the number of skiers or even the stunning snow-covered landscape, though it was incredibly picturesque; it was the dedication of the ski lift operators. They performed their duties with such care— swiping snowflakes off each seat and ensuring no snow built up on the landings—even though few people were around to notice. Their commitment to the task was inspiring. It wasn't about recognition; it was about honouring their work, no matter how small.

Similarly, whenever we asked locals for directions, they wouldn't just point the way; they would take us all the way to our destination. Once, in Tokyo Disneyland, we asked a group of four young girls, all dressed identically in fluffy white leg warmers and pink Minnie Mouse headbands, where a food stand was. Rather than merely pointing us in the right direction, they insisted on walking us to the dagwood dog stand. It took nearly ten minutes, but their politeness, honour and generosity were remarkable.

It was in these moments that I saw ikigai come to life. Whether through their work or everyday interactions, the Japanese approach their lives with purpose and intention, finding meaning in even the smallest actions. I returned home with a deep desire to bring that same sense of dedication and purpose into my own life and work.

Ever since, I've woven ikigai into how I think about purpose, fulfilment, and how we can all live more meaningful lives. It's not just about grand, sweeping goals or accumulating financial wealth. It's about how we show up for ourselves and others in seemingly small moments.

As you continue through this chapter, I encourage you to reflect on the idea of ikigai and how it might apply to your own life. What is your reason for getting up in the morning? How can you align your values, passions, talents and contributions to create a life filled with joy and meaning?

Let's turn the focus back to you. With your growing self-worth and a new awareness of your limiting beliefs, it's time to uncover your values and begin finding your purpose.

In this book, purpose refers to your personal life mission or ikigai. Ikigai and purpose are similar in many ways; both involve finding meaning and fulfilment in life. The Japanese concept of ikigai translates to 'a reason for being' or 'a reason to wake up in the morning'. Likewise, in Eastern philosophy, the concept of Dharma refers to living in alignment with your true nature and fulfilling your responsibilities in the world. Together, these ideas emphasise a life lived with intention and alignment.

So, how do you find your purpose, ikigai, or Dharma, and is there only one?

This chapter will delve into your core values before exploring your life purpose. Just like acknowledging your limiting beliefs helps to inform your belief affirmation, knowing your core values will help inform your life purpose, like the keys to different gates in a secret garden.

I first encountered the concept of ikigai while watching the Netflix series *Secrets of the Blue Zones*, where Dan Buettner, the author of *The Blue Zones: Lessons for Living Longer from the People Who've Lived the Longest*, travels the world to discover five unique communities where people live extraordinarily long and vibrant lives.

In Okinawa, Japan, Dan discovered that Okinawans have a strong sense of purpose in life, a driving force they call ikigai. Buettner notes, 'The secret to longevity lies in the very concept of ikigai. It is the thing that gets you up in the morning.'

Ikigai represents the intersection of what you love, what you are good at, what the world needs, and what you can be paid for. Similarly, purpose refers to the reason something is done or created, often implying a sense of direction, meaning or significance.

Both ikigai and purpose involve understanding oneself— your passions, talents, and how you can contribute to the world. They emphasise living a fulfilling and meaningful life, aligning with your values and aspirations. While career success or financial goals can be part of your purpose, true fulfilment comes from living in alignment with what matters most to you in the overall scheme of things.

Your Core Values

You might be wondering why personal core values are so important. Personal core values are the guiding principles that represent your unique essence. They shape your actions, behaviours and decisions, acting like an internal compass that directs you towards your authentic self. Living in alignment with your values enhances your sense of self and contributes to mental wellbeing, helping you feel more content, fulfilled and at peace.

I delved into the importance of values while studying life coaching with Kain Ramsey through Achology: The Academy of Modern Applied Psychology, and under the mentorship of Bernard Kates, a transformational leadership coach. Through this experience, I learned that we feel authentic, connected and grounded when we live in harmony with our values. These values guide us personally and inform how we manage our relationships, careers, time and finances. They act as a foundation for growth, appreciation, and protection of the things that matter most to us.

In moments when our choices deviate from our core values, we can feel frustrated, dissatisfied or resentful. Awareness of our values helps us understand why certain people or situations may trigger us because they don't align with what we believe is true and right. By recognising this, we can become more curious rather than reactive, allowing us to approach challenging situations with understanding. Taking time to uncover your core values is essential.

Set aside some quiet time for this exercise, ideally thirty to forty-five minutes. Find a comfortable place to sit with your journal or blank paper.

Step 1—Reflect on Positive Moments

- Reflect on a moment when you felt happy, fulfilled and proud.

- Describe what you were doing, if you were with other people and anything else that contributed to these feelings.

Step 2—Reflect on Negative Moments

- Journal about a moment when you felt regretful, frustrated, empty or annoyed.

- What led to these feelings for you? There may be more than one moment you wish to journal on.

Step 3—Identify Activities That Bring Joy

- Make a list of activities you enjoy that cause you to get into a state of flow. Flow refers to the mental state where you become fully immersed and absorbed in an activity. In this state, you often lose track of time because the task is both engaging and challenging enough to hold your focus. Flow activities typically require skill but provide enjoyment, making them rewarding as well as stimulating. Think about when you've felt so engaged in something that hours seemed to pass in what felt like minutes—that's flow.

- What is it about these activities that brings you so much flow and joy? Some examples may be painting, reading, writing, a particular exercise such as running or weights, cooking, gardening, playing an instrument, solving a complex puzzle, and so on.

Step 4—Reflect on Role Models

• Reflect on your role models, the people you admire, and their specific qualities. This could be family members, sports-people, friends, colleagues, movie stars, politicians—anyone. Think about what draws you to these individuals—whether it's their compassion, determination, leadership or creativity.

• Often, the qualities we admire in others are a reflection of the traits we have within ourselves. These role models serve as mirrors, showing us our own potential. When we see strength, courage or kindness in others, it's because we recognise and value these traits in ourselves, even if we haven't fully embraced them yet.

Step 5—Acknowledge Your Natural Gifts

• Acknowledge your natural gifts and qualities.

• What do people usually turn to you for? In other words, how do others find value in you?

Step 6—Compile and Prioritise Your Values

• Use the list of examples of core values in Figure 2 below. Based on your answers and reflections, aim to write a list of approximately twenty values. Group similar values until you can prioritise your top three to five values.

FIGURE 2 List of Core Values

Uncovering your core values helps you gain clarity on what truly matters to you. These values are central to your identity and shape the person you want to become. This deeper awareness fosters curiosity and acceptance in your relationships and experiences, particularly in moments of discomfort or conflict. Additionally, knowing and recalling your core values aids decision-making, allowing you to prioritise what you value most and ultimately create a genuinely worthy and wealthy life for yourself.

CLIENT STORY

Kelyn was a client of mine for over a year. She initially contacted me for life coaching because she had trouble completing her studies to become a private investigator. At sixty-nine years old, Kelyn worked part-time in social work and was contemplating retirement. She wanted something that would keep her occupied and fulfilled when that time came. Kelyn struggled with procrastination, and during our time together she faced additional hurdles, including the passing of her husband, who had been battling lymphoma.

In our second session, we worked through Kelyn's values, which we narrowed down to family, contribution, purpose and justice as her core motivators.

By continually revisiting these values throughout our sessions, Kelyn discovered that they were more than just guiding principles—they were intrinsic to her identity. She realised how much her desire to connect missing people with their families aligned with her value of justice and contribution. These values, inherited from her own family, had shaped her life's work in social services and were now leading her towards a new path as a private investigator. Despite the obstacles of grief and procrastination, Kelyn's values served as an anchor, helping her navigate difficult moments and giving her the resolve to press on when life became overwhelming.

After eighteen months of persistence, Kelyn successfully completed her final assessment and earned her Certificate III in Investigations. Life may have thrown many challenges her way, but her core values sustained her, helping her continue her quest to connect missing people. Through this process, Kelyn gained new skills and continued to live out her purpose of making a difference in people's lives, even beyond retirement. Ultimately, her journey was less about the qualification and more about staying connected to what truly mattered to her, which brought her fulfilment and a renewed sense of purpose in her life.

Journal Prompt—Value Statement

You can use your values to form a value statement or even an affirmation that may support you as you navigate life. Consider creating a value statement that includes all your values. For instance, if your values are focused on connection, belonging, creativity, legacy or authenticity, like mine, you can create a value statement that includes those ideas. For example, 'I am deeply connected to the world around me, fostering meaningful relationships that nurture my sense of belonging and authenticity. With creativity as my guide, I leave a legacy of inspiration and innovation, shaping a future built on love, purpose, and genuine connection with others.'

Using tools like AI can be very helpful for generating ideas and curating a statement that aligns with you. Alternatively, you can play with the words yourself.

Remember, your core beliefs and values may shift throughout your life. Depending on your circumstances, some will become more important than others at different times. They are not fixed, so you may want to revisit both exercises occasionally.

Finding Your Purpose

As I've explored the concept of purpose while writing this book and speaking with others, I've noticed how it naturally shifts throughout different stages of life. Early on, purpose often revolves around education, career and financial stability. For mothers, particularly in the early years of parenthood, purpose is often tied to their children's needs and the adventure of raising a family.

As we approach midlife, when financial concerns may ease and children grow more independent, purpose tends to shift again. It becomes more about personal fulfilment and deeper connections beyond our roles. This stage invites reflection: who are we beyond our responsibilities? What impact do we want to have on the world? Ikigai and Dharma provide meaningful frameworks for this reflection, helping us explore how to align our passions, talents and values with the greater good—creating a life that is not only purposeful but also deeply fulfilling.

For me, defining my purpose has been an evolving journey centred around fostering meaningful relationships and promoting authenticity. Guided by creativity, I aim to leave a legacy of inspiration, innovation, and connection. My purpose is to create, connect, explore and inspire, leaving a lasting positive impact on others.

Now it's your turn. Take some time to reflect on your purpose through the following prompts and begin crafting your own purpose statement.

Step 1—Reflect on Your Impact on Others

- Think about actions you take that positively impact others' lives.

- Reflect on what people typically seek your help for or express gratitude towards you for.

- Imagine yourself teaching others; what valuable lessons or skills would you impart?

Step 2—Identify Activities Where You Find Fulfilment and Flow

- What tasks bring you a deep sense of fulfilment, regardless of compensation?

- Consider activities that engross you so deeply that time seems to disappear.

- What are your natural strengths or talents, and how do they align with your sense of purpose?

Step 3—Reflect on Your Non-Negotiable Actions

- What actions would you take even if they made you appear foolish to others?

- Think about moments where you stood by your values, even at a cost.

Step 4—Recall Memories from Your Childhood

- Reflect on activities that brought you joy in your childhood and why they mattered to you.

- Recall your happiest childhood memory and what made it so special.

Step 5—Prioritise What is Most Important to You

- Imagine how you would spend your time if you had only one year to live.

- Define success on your own terms. How does your purpose align with this vision of success?

These prompts are designed to help you gain deeper insight into your purpose, which often aligns closely with your values and your heart's deepest desires. Take your time with each prompt, jotting down thoughts and reflections as they arise. Also, consider exploring any limiting beliefs that may be holding you back from fully embracing your purpose. How can you reframe these beliefs to foster growth?

Journal Prompt—Crafting Your Purpose Statement

Once you've reflected on these prompts, use the insights gained to craft your purpose statement. Similar to your Value Statement, this is a guiding statement for your life, rooted in your core values and personal goals. Feel free to use tools like AI to explore different versions of your statement or simply journal until you find one that truly resonates with you.

THOUGH JULES WAS gaining a clearer sense of direction, she knew the road ahead would still be filled with challenges and discoveries, particularly in her relationships and daily experiences. Yet, with her newfound emotional clarity and connection to her values, she felt more equipped than ever to face these challenges with curiosity and compassion rather than fear or avoidance. Her deeper understanding of belonging, empathy and vitality made her interactions with others richer and more meaningful, helping her respond to situations from a place of calm and purpose instead of falling into old reactive patterns.

In particular, her relationship with her ex-husband, Dean, had become noticeably less volatile. Jules began to recognise how their conflicting values had led to past friction, and this newfound awareness helped her understand why they had triggered each other so deeply. She was also much calmer at home, so her relationships with her children blossomed. Jules felt more connected than ever to herself and others, radiating that sense of peace throughout her life.

As Jules reflected on her core values and her growing desire for personal and professional development, a seed of purpose began to take root. Her deep enjoyment of her role at the psychology practice only strengthened her resolve, inspiring her to take her passion further. Studying psychology seemed like the natural next step; it aligned with her love of helping others and her desire to make a broader impact. With excitement, she began researching university programs, visualising a future where she thrived both personally and professionally as a practising psychologist.

This newfound clarity echoed the Japanese concept of ikigai—a reason for being. For Jules, her ikigai was beginning to take shape as a harmonious blend of what she loved, what she was good at, what the world needed, and what she could be rewarded for. Each day, she took a step closer to embodying this balance, pursuing her passions while finding joy and meaning in the journey.

Like Jules, your purpose may unfold slowly, but with every small step you take, you'll move closer to living your ikigai. Let each exercise in this chapter serve as a key to unlocking the gates of your own secret garden, guiding you towards a life of harmony, joy and meaning.

Now that Jules had more clarity about what she wanted, the next step was to figure out the path that would lead her to her long-term goal.

AS WE WRAP UP this chapter, take a moment to acknowledge the significant strides you've made by engaging with the exercises. While obstacles, like the limiting beliefs uncovered in Chapter 1, might still arise, your newfound awareness allows you to challenge these beliefs and realign with your path, one step at a time. It's essential to notice these internal shifts as they occur, reflecting and journaling on your thoughts and feelings regularly.

Let this sense of purpose guide you forward, acting as both your compass and your fuel for the future chapters ahead.

CHAPTER HIGHLIGHTS

- **The concept of ikigai**: Ikigai represents the harmonious intersection of what you love, what you're good at, what the world needs, and what you can be rewarded for. It's about finding your personal life mission and living with purpose, fulfilment and joy—it's your reason to get up in the morning.

- **Purpose is an evolving journey**: Your sense of purpose may shift throughout different stages of life, but by staying connected to your values and passions, you can continuously cultivate a life filled with meaning and abundance.

- **The power of core values**: Uncovering and understanding your core values is essential to living an authentic, fulfilling life. These values act as a compass, guiding your decisions, relationships and overall wellbeing.

- **Journaling and reflection**: Regular journaling and reflection on your values, purpose and limiting beliefs provide clarity and help you overcome obstacles. This practice supports personal growth and keeps you aligned with your true self.

- **The importance of small steps**: Finding and living your ikigai or Dharma is a gradual process. Every small step you take, like Jules, brings you closer to embodying your purpose and creating a life of harmony, joy and fulfilment.

3

NECTAR

I AM WELL

The single most important factor influencing your wellbeing and personal fulfilment is your ability to take care of your own needs.

CHERYL RICHARDSON
author of *The Art of Extreme Self-Care*

As MENTIONED IN Chapter 2, Jules' life coach, Amanda, encouraged her to start journaling and meditating. Jules found journaling easy; it brought her back to her younger days when she kept a diary and even journaled during her backpacking adventures in her twenties. But life, with all its responsibilities and the demands of family, had pushed journaling to the back burner over the years.

Meditation, however, was another story. Jules found it much harder. She felt like she was doing it all wrong, with her mind buzzing louder than ever when she tried to sit still. The endless to-do lists, dinner, groceries, bills, Jimmy's school forms and buying new shoes always flooded her thoughts, making it almost unbearable. At first, she could only manage a minute before giving up.

Amanda reassured her that there was no right or wrong way to meditate. She reminded Jules that the key was to notice her thoughts with curiosity, and when they became overwhelming, to gently guide herself back to her breath. Amanda also suggested using the Insight Timer app for guided meditations, which turned out to be a game changer for Jules.

In the beginning, Jules only managed to meditate and journal a few times a week. Her busy mornings at She Fit still had her blasting out of bed. Amanda suggested a softer approach: setting her alarm just fifteen minutes earlier to allow time for a quick meditation, journaling, and writing down three things she was grateful for each day.

Practising gratitude didn't come easily at first. Jules struggled to think of unique things to be thankful for. But something soon shifted—she began consciously seeking out things to appreciate throughout her day. It became a small but powerful way to manage stress, redirect her focus and nurture her wellbeing.

As the days went by, Jules started to look forward to her morning practice. She grew curious about what thoughts would surface during meditation, which she could later explore in her journal. Her journal became a trusted confidante where she could work through the emotions stirred up by her coaching sessions and her everyday life.

Through this practice, Jules learned patience with herself. Instead of berating herself for struggling with meditation or feeling overwhelmed, she began to practise self-compassion. She gave herself permission to be imperfect and to accept that slowing down was part of the process. As she embraced these small but significant changes, she noticed a newfound sense of calm in the mornings, which flowed into her entire day. Even the hustle of getting the kids to school and herself to work felt more manageable.

WHAT DOES WELLBEING have to do with worth or wealth?

Becoming intentional about your wellbeing is a cornerstone for deepening your sense of self, and this naturally feeds into your sense of worth. When you prioritise your health, you're sending a strong message to yourself and the world that you are valuable and deserving of care. This, in turn, is linked to wealth not just in a financial sense but in the richness of your life experiences, relationships and overall fulfilment.

In this chapter, we'll break down three vital areas of wellbeing: nurturing your body, stimulating your mind, and the critical importance of getting quality sleep. It's widely accepted among health professionals that while exercise plays a crucial role in maintaining overall health, diet tends to have a more significant impact on your health outcomes. This is an important insight, as many people tend to focus heavily on exercise when real progress often starts in the kitchen.[1]

We'll also explore how creating a consistent morning or evening routine can support your self-care and help replenish your energy. Along the way, we'll talk about the importance of positive and nourishing relationships and experiences, as these are an essential component of wellbeing that contribute to a richer, more fulfilled life.

Your Wellness Routine

I heard whisperings of meditation, journaling and practising gratitude for years, but like many people, life always seemed

---

1   https://www.mayoclinic.org/healthy-lifestyle/weight-loss/in-depth/weight-loss/art-20047752

too busy to fit them in. While I had kept a journal on and off throughout my life due to my love of writing, I found that as my career and family responsibilities grew, journaling fell away. Life sped up, and autopilot kicked in.

But when life gets crazy—whether it's a job change, a divorce, a pandemic, or the challenges of raising teenage kids—there are always basic things we can do to improve our wellbeing. Think of these as your wellbeing tool kit and consistency as key. Without it, we risk turning to food and drink to numb our painful feelings, which only offers temporary relief and often leaves us feeling worse.

As predictable human beings with similar needs, it's safe to say that we all require some basic things like exercise, sleep and mental stimulation. You can think of it as the nectar that provides the butterfly energy and good health.

Step 1—Taking Care of Your Body

Let's begin with how you nourish your physical body from a hydration and diet perspective. They say you are what you eat, and I've always done my best to fuel my body adequately. My early interest in nutrition began many years ago when I came across *You Are What You Eat* by Dr Gillian McKeith. Although her ideas sparked my curiosity and initial education on the topic, over time I explored other sources and broadened my understanding of nutrition, delving into more scientifically grounded approaches.

One of my mantras, passed on to me from my mum, is 'everything in moderation'. I'm not about to start spruiking the latest diet to you; we are all educated enough these days to make the right choices for our unique bodies. And that's the key—our unique bodies. We each have different shapes, metabolisms and genetic makeups. Even when we do everything in our power to be as healthy as possible, our bodies may look different from what we see in others. Believe me,

I've had my fair share of not loving my body as much as I could at different points in my life. But I've learned that self-acceptance of how we physically look is integral to our overall wellbeing and, ultimately, our self-worth. Nourishing our bodies isn't just about what we eat or how we move; it's also about embracing our physical selves with kindness and gratitude for all that they allow us to be and do in the world.

I don't categorise food as 'good' or 'bad'. It's just food. I've learned to listen to my body intuitively. If I deny myself, I'm more likely to binge, so I allow myself to enjoy small portions of indulgent foods while prioritising those that nourish and fuel my body for the long term. Simple practices like eating the rainbow and having smaller meat portions balanced with plenty of salads and vegetables (even though I'm not particularly fond of some vegetables) help me make informed, sustainable choices.

Over the years, I've gained more knowledge about healthy eating, and the 80/20 food rule has become a helpful guide for me: eighty percent of the time, I focus on consuming nutritious, whole foods that support my health, while the remaining twenty percent allows for flexibility and indulgence without too much guilt. This balanced approach helps me maintain a healthy and sustainable relationship with food. Chocolate, for instance, remains one of my all-time favourites—I'm just more into dark chocolate these days.

Drinking enough water is just as essential for overall health. The general guideline is to consume around 2.5 litres (about ten cups) of water per day for men and around 2 litres (about eight cups) for women.[2] Staying hydrated is crucial for digestion, energy levels, avoiding headaches, and supporting our overall wellbeing.

---

2   https://www.healthdirect.gov.au/drinking-water-and-your-health

Physical activity has always been important to me. Moving my body for at least thirty minutes four times a week has been an essential practice of mine for as long as I can remember. This practice has kept me feeling fit and healthy. As I entered early menopause in my mid-forties, I became even more aware of the importance of muscle-strengthening activities to support bone density, maintain muscle mass, and balance hormones during this transition. Strength training, especially for women in perimenopause and menopause, is essential in preventing muscle loss and improving metabolic health.

The Australian Institute of Health and Welfare recommends that adults engage in at least 150 minutes of moderate physical activity per week, including muscle-strengthening activities such as lifting weights, Pilates and yoga, to maintain good health and wellbeing.[3] This statistic underscores the importance of integrating regular exercise into your routine for a balanced and fulfilling life. Additionally, it's important to minimise and break up prolonged periods of sitting. I've even taken this advice to heart by writing this book at a stand-up desk, ensuring that I stay active and avoid long stretches of inactivity.

My physical activity generally consists of two outdoor walks per week, two weight and cardio sessions at the gym, and a home yoga class. I also enjoy stretching with bands and weights while watching television a couple of times per week. This level of activity works for me—it helps me maintain a healthy weight range, muscle tone and flexibility, and provides enough endorphins to keep me strong and happy; plus, the outdoor walks and being in nature are so good for my soul. What this looks like for you may be different, but

---

3   https://www.aihw.gov.au/reports/physical-activity/physical-activity

studies show that a similar routine benefits overall health. I also love working out with my daughters and friends, which adds a social connection to taking care of my body—an added bonus I cherish.

Step 2—Exercising Your Mind

As much as they say you are what you eat, it's equally true that you are what you think. Your thoughts shape your reality. While maintaining a healthy body is important, mental health can often be overlooked, especially when life gets busy. There's also a growing body of research suggesting that the gut is like a second brain, emphasising the mind-body connection even further. However, exercising the mind and nurturing our mental health is often the first thing we let slide. It's easy to get caught up in mindless activities like binge-watching Netflix or endlessly scrolling through social media, which may seem relaxing but often contribute negatively to comparison and, ultimately, our mental wellbeing.

When the pandemic hit, and I found myself in the throes of perimenopause while raising teenagers, life became overwhelming. This period forced me to reassess the habits I had fallen into. I finally decided to take control by downloading the Insight Timer app and sporadically meditating, hoping to find some peace of mind. I also found a simple A5 notepad and began journaling my thoughts and practising gratitude by writing down three things I was thankful for, and I began to feel different.

It was a feeling of calmness that I had not experienced for a long time. This newfound serenity allowed me to respond with more patience and understanding towards my partner and family. I became less reactive and more thoughtful. By giving myself time and space, new thoughts and ideas began to surface about the bigger picture, not just what I had to do that day or that week.

One of the most effective ways to nurture your mind is through mindfulness and intentional thinking. By paying attention to the quality of your thoughts and making space for reflection, you create the mental clarity necessary for growth and creativity. Just like you wouldn't expect your body to be strong without exercise, your mind also needs intentional care and attention to remain healthy and resilient.

The American Psychological Association defines mindfulness as 'awareness of one's internal states and surroundings. Mindfulness can help people avoid destructive or automatic habits and responses by learning to observe their thoughts, emotions and other present-moment experiences without judging or reacting to them.'[4]

Adding mindfulness exercises like meditation, journaling, gratitude practice and breathing techniques to your routine is an excellent way to nurture mental wellbeing. It's also important to recognise when your thoughts might be leading you into a negative spiral and to be kind to yourself during difficult moments. If you struggle with this, then think about treating yourself like you would a friend.

Step 3—Getting Your Beauty Sleep

A crucial aspect of wellbeing is sleep. According to the National Sleep Foundation, adults need between seven and nine hours of sleep per night to function optimally.[5] I advocate for a more intuitive approach to sleep.

Speaking from experience, I tried the 5 am morning routine for years, and while it served me well when my children were young and my husband left early for work, it took its

---

4 https://www.apa.org/topics/mindfulness

5 https://www.thensf.org/how-many-hours-of-sleep-do-you-really-need/

toll. Sometimes, the alarm went off at 4:40 am, and I felt utterly exhausted. As much as I tried to go to bed early, it just didn't happen. Sometimes, that 4:40 am alarm meant I was only getting around five hours of sleep, which is insufficient for anyone to function optimally.

A good rule of thumb is to work backwards from when you want to wake up. Aiming for around seven hours of sleep is just enough; eight is ideal, and six is functional but barely sustainable as a routine. So, if you want to get up at 5 am, then be asleep by 10 pm at the latest, or if 7 am is your wake-up time, you need to be asleep by midnight. And when I say asleep, I don't mean lying in bed scrolling through Instagram. I've learned that reading or meditating before bed helps me relax and drift off faster, leading to better-quality rest.

Finding your natural sleep pattern is all about tuning in to your body's signals. Try going to bed earlier and avoiding screens for at least an hour before you settle in. It takes time to develop a new sleep habit, so be patient with yourself. If a particular routine doesn't feel right after some time, adjust it until you find something that works for you. Pay attention to how easily you fall asleep and how refreshed you feel in the morning. The infamous 3 pm energy slump might also indicate that you aren't getting enough quality sleep.

Learning my natural sleeping patterns has been key to showing up as the best version of myself, and the next step has been developing a morning routine. As I mentioned earlier, I start my day with a short meditation, journaling and gratitude practice, which takes as little as ten minutes. This small routine sets a positive tone for my day.

A recent article from Charles Sturt University highlights the benefits of incorporating mindfulness into a morning routine. It explains that 'engaging in activities like meditation, deep breathing, or yoga during your morning routine promotes emotional self-awareness and helps manage stress."[6] Though not a formal study, this perspective aligns with growing evidence that supports the positive impact of mindful morning practices on mental and physical wellbeing.

If you know you're not a morning person, or you're in a different life stage—perhaps with young children who dictate your wake-up time—it's essential to honour who you are, and the season you're in. Don't feel pressured to wake up at 5 am if it's not working for you. You might prefer to switch your mindfulness practice to the evening instead.

Self-Care and Nourishment

As I became more consistent with my gratitude practice, journaling in general, and meditation, I felt more grounded and present. I had more clarity and perspective in my life. Taking this time to go inward and self-reflect was transformational, and I slowly added more mindfulness practices to my daily ritual.

Embracing the wellbeing practices outlined in this chapter has not only improved my daily life, but also helped me navigate the challenges of perimenopause and menopause with greater ease. By prioritising self-care and mindfulness, I've gained resilience and emotional balance during this transitional phase. Resilience, after all, is about moving forward despite adversity. Like many, I faced significant challenges during the pandemic, along with navigating my children's health issues and the effects of perimenopause. Yet, through it all, I managed to continue transforming my life thanks to intentionally practising mindfulness.

---

6   https://charlie.csu.edu.au/2023/10/26/the-power-of-a-morning-routine-a-psychological-perspective/

And the ripple effect is real. By prioritising self-care, you become a role model for those around you. If you're a mum like me, you want to set an example for your children that prioritising wellbeing is essential. When you model self-care, you demonstrate that it's not selfish but a path to unconditional self-love.

Self-care can take many different forms for different people, and it's crucial to recognise that what works for one person might not be the best approach for another. For instance, the kind of rest and rejuvenation needed by someone with a physically demanding job might be different from that of someone with a desk job. The former might find true rest in unwinding with Netflix, while the latter might feel more nourished by jogging or engaging in physical activity. Understanding the diversity of self-care practices, whether it's through physical activities like Jules' dance classes, mental relaxation, spiritual practices, or even a digital detox if you find yourself in comparison paralysis, allows us to meet our unique needs more effectively. True rest, nourishment and healing go beyond just meeting basic needs; they are about discovering what genuinely recharges and restores us, tailored to our individual circumstances and lifestyles.

Journal Prompt—Self-Care

Self-care is a deeply personal practice that can take many different forms, depending on your unique needs and lifestyle. As we've explored in this chapter, true rest, nourishment and healing can be found in various ways: through quiet reflection, physical activity or creative expression. The key is to discover what genuinely replenishes your energy and nurtures your wellbeing.

Step 1—Reflect on the Impact of Your Self-Care Routine

- Reflect on a time when prioritising your wellbeing made a noticeable difference in your day. How did it affect your mood, energy and interactions with others?

Step 2—Select Self-Care Activities to Prioritise

- Choose three self-care activities from the following list (or create your own) that resonate with you and that you would like to incorporate into your daily or weekly routine. Here are some ideas:

  - Take a bath
  - Go for a walk in nature
  - Read a book
  - Listen to music
  - Watch your favourite TV show or movie
  - Write in a journal
  - Declutter your living space
  - Pamper yourself with a long shower and facial
  - Take a nap
  - Plant flowers in your garden
  - Cook a healthy meal or try a new recipe
  - Try a new workout
  - Watch the sunrise or sunset
  - Try a new craft or hobby
  - Try a new coffee or tea
  - Buy yourself a treat
  - Take a day off from work
  - Take a break from social media
  - Learn a new dance routine
  - Attend a meditation or sound healing class

Step 3—Journal About Modelling Self-Care for Others

- Consider how you can model self-care for those around you. How does demonstrating self-love and care impact your relationships, especially with your children, partner, family or close friends?

Step 4—Reflect on the Results

- After a week, revisit your journal to reflect on any changes you've noticed in your mood, energy levels or overall sense of wellbeing. Have you observed any shifts in how you feel or how you interact with others?

CLIENT STORY

Terri, a full-time working mother, felt overwhelmed by the demands of her career and home life, even though she shared the load with her partner. She reached out to me, seeking guidance to help her navigate these challenges and reclaim her sense of self-worth and balance.

During our sessions, we focused on recognising her worth and strengths, which had become clouded by the pressures of daily life. Through tailored discussions and exercises, Terri began to see her true value and the importance of prioritising her wellbeing.

Terri's transformation was profound. She moved up in her career, finding new confidence and clarity in her professional role. Her home environment became happier and more harmonious as she applied the principles we discussed. Most importantly, she shed the guilt associated with making time for herself, realising that self-care was not a luxury but a necessity.

Terri found a new sense of balance and fulfilment by consistently incorporating wellbeing practices, such as physical movement, meditation, journaling and setting healthy boundaries, into her life. The change wasn't immediate; it came with tears, fears and moments of unease, but through persistence and self-compassion, Terri created a happier, more harmonious life. The ripple effect was real. As Terri poured more love and attention into herself, it radiated throughout her life, positively impacting her family and career.

Terri continues to stay in touch, often sharing updates on her journey. She is now a happy single mother, thriving in a healthy co-parenting relationship, and a proud first-time homeowner. Her story is a powerful testament to the transformative impact of recognising one's worth and prioritising wellbeing. Her experience inspires others in similar situations, showing that significant positive changes are possible with the right mindset and guidance.

Feed Your Soul

When reflecting on wellbeing, it's easy to overlook how deeply our sense of connection impacts us. Yet, meaningful relationships are at the heart of a truly fulfilling life. These enriching connections—whether with family, friends, colleagues or mentors—are vital to our overall wellbeing.

Even when we're surrounded by others, it's not uncommon to feel a sense of loneliness, a stark reminder that true connection is about depth, not just proximity. Fostering meaningful relationships is essential for our wellbeing and is a fundamental pillar in creating a truly wealthy life.

Much of our joy stems from shared and enriching experiences with significant others, be it family holidays, nights out with friends, or simple moments of quality time. Strong, supportive, inspiring, charismatic and kind connections bring immense joy and fulfilment, enhancing our overall wellbeing and boosting our self-worth.

While it's essential to foster positive connections, it's equally important to recognise when certain relationships no longer serve your wellbeing. This is particularly challenging when it comes to family or long-standing friendships, where there may be a sense of obligation or history that makes it difficult to step back. However, it's crucial to prioritise your mental and emotional health. If you find that a relationship consistently drains your energy, causes stress, or leads to feelings of inadequacy, it may be time to re-evaluate its place in your life.

You might start by setting boundaries. This could mean limiting the time you spend with these individuals or deciding on specific topics that are off-limits during conversations. Boundaries are not about shutting people out but protecting your peace and ensuring that your interactions are healthy and respectful.

In some cases, distancing yourself might be necessary. This can be done gradually by reducing the frequency of contact or choosing to spend more time with people who have a positive impact on your life. Letting go of a toxic relationship can be an act of self-care and self-respect. It's about making room for connections that truly nourish you and contribute to your growth. And while it might not be easy, it's often necessary to maintain your overall wellbeing and peace of mind.

In the workplace, where we often have less control over who we interact with daily, it's important to find strategies to protect your energy. If a boss or colleague consistently brings negativity or stress into your life, consider setting clearer boundaries, limiting unnecessary interactions or addressing the issue constructively.

They say you are the sum of the five people you spend the most time with, so surround yourself with those who encourage and uplift you. This will cultivate an environment that nourishes your soul and enhances every aspect of your wellbeing.

Journal Prompt—Feed Your Soul

Reflect on the role of meaningful connections in your life and how they impact your wellbeing. Consider both the enriching relationships that uplift and nourish you, as well as those that may drain your energy.

Step 1—Reflect on Positive Connections
- Write about a time when a meaningful connection with someone positively impacted your day. How did it affect your mood, energy and overall wellbeing?

Step 2—Identifying and Setting Boundaries with Negative Connections
- Consider relationships or connections that might negatively affect your wellbeing. What makes them challenging for you? Reflect on your unique values and how theirs may differ. After identifying these challenging relationships, journal about how you can set healthy boundaries to protect your energy. Are there steps you can take to limit time spent or to reframe how you engage in these relationships?

Step 3—Fostering Healthier Relationships

- Think about the relationships you want to nurture. How can you prioritise spending more time with people who support and inspire you? Choose three self-care and enriching activities that foster connection from the list below (or create your own) that resonate with you and that you would like to incorporate into your daily or weekly routine to foster more positive connection. Here are some ideas:

  - Calling a friend
  - Going to the gym with a friend or group
  - Spending time with a loved one
  - Taking a yoga class
  - Having a picnic in the park with friends
  - Listening to a podcast
  - Spending time with animals
  - Getting a massage
  - Doing a puzzle or playing a board game with others
  - Going to the beach or a lake
  - Having a cosy movie night at home with the kids
  - Joining a book club
  - Creating a self-care playlist with your and your friends' favourite songs
  - Going for a bike ride or taking a spin class
  - Going for a long lunch with your friends
  - Visiting a museum or art gallery with family
  - Date night

Step 4—Reflecting on the Impact

- Journaling is crucial as it allows you to track your progress and reflect on any improvements in your overall wellbeing over the week. Write down your completed activities and note how they made you feel throughout the day. Observe any shifts in how you feel or how you interact with others. After a week, revisit your journal and reflect on any changes you've noticed in your mood or energy. Have you observed any shifts in how your positive or negative relationships affect your wellbeing?

You can also download a free 7-Day Self-Care Challenge from my website for extra self-care ideas and accountability at www.emmalagerlow.com/7-day-self-care-challenge.

THE COMBINATION OF daily morning practices and an improved sleep routine allowed Jules to feel more focused and clear-minded. No longer weighed down by the mental clutter and constant comparison that once overwhelmed her, she was able to prioritise what truly mattered—her health and relationships.

Around this time, Jules had a massive 'aha' moment when she discovered she was in perimenopause, which likely contributed to the insomnia and other ailments mentioned in Chapter 1. With healthier and more balanced lifestyle choices, she was able to manage her symptoms with greater ease. Regular consultations with her GP and an openness to medical support, including hormone replacement therapy, gave her a reassuring sense of control over her wellbeing.

Her commitment to moving her body most mornings, coupled with a mindful approach to diet and hydration, elevated her physical health to new heights. Jules noticed fewer aches and pains, enjoyed higher energy levels, and embraced her physical appearance with newfound positivity, appreciating her body for all it does for her.

Regular meditation and gratitude practices deepened her sense of inner peace. She felt more grounded, less reactive to stress, and found joy in the simple things. Her journaling practice became a sanctuary where she processed thoughts and emotions, building greater emotional resilience.

As Jules deepened her self-care practices, she also became more discerning in her relationships, understanding that the quality of her connections directly influences her wellbeing. Through reflection on her relationships and the space she's given herself to go inward, Jules became more attuned to which connections uplift her and which ones drain her energy. Establishing better boundaries around who she spends time with contributed to her sense of grounding and emotional stability.

As a result of her self-care practices, Jules was better equipped to handle life's challenges. She approached obstacles with her ex-husband, her children, colleagues, family and friends with a calm mind and a heart full of gratitude, knowing she had the tools to maintain her wellbeing regardless of external circumstances.

Jules was now in a much stronger and more centred place. She was not only aware of but wholly embraced her evolving midlife stage and developed a daily routine that nourished her mind, body and soul. This holistic approach to her wellbeing brought her a newfound sense of peace, purpose and connection to those around her.

CHAPTER HIGHLIGHTS

- **Prioritising self-care:** This chapter emphasises the importance of caring for your needs as a cornerstone of wellbeing. This includes caring for your body through proper hydration, eating nourishing food using the 80/20 rule, and getting enough sleep and regular physical activity.

- **Balance the mind/body connection:** Nurturing your mind is just as crucial as caring for your body. Just as physical strength requires exercise, your mind needs dedicated care to remain healthy and resilient. This chapter explores the importance of cultivating resilience through mindfulness practices like meditation, journaling and gratitude.

- **Self-care practices are unique:** Self-care is deeply personal and individualised and can take many forms depending on your unique needs and lifestyle. Whether through quiet reflection, physical activity or creative expression, this chapter encourages you to explore and discover self-care practices that nourish your energy and nurture your wellbeing. Remember to be flexible with your self-care routine as your needs and circumstances evolve over time.

- **Cultivating enriching relationships and experiences:** Building and maintaining enriching relationships is vital for your wellbeing. This chapter explores the importance of being in tune with your values and regularly checking in with what feels meaningful for you in your relationships. Doing so allows you to cultivate positive connections and set strong boundaries, using effective communication to protect your wellbeing. Limiting time with or removing connections that consistently bring negativity into your life can be a powerful act of self-care.

- **The ripple effect of self-care:** Prioritising your wellbeing enhances your life and positively impacts those around you. This chapter illustrates the power of modelling self-care for others and how it can create a more harmonious and fulfilling environment in your relationships and community.

4

WINGS

I AM WEALTHY

Financial results are a part of wealth, but there are so many other parts of feeling wealthy and abundant.

LAETITIA ANDRAC
business doula, Essential Shift

ET'S REVISIT our friend Jules to see how she was going five years after we were last in her orbit. She had begun studying psychology and was four years into the course with aspirations of becoming a clinical psychologist and buying into the private practice where she worked. She loved every minute of her time in the nurturing and enriching workplace, and formed strong relationships with her colleagues.

A couple of years into her life change, Jules had invested in a beautiful apartment close to the beach. On the surface, it seemed like a dream come true. She was living in a place she adored, so close to the ocean she loved. However, behind the scenes, Jules often found herself juggling financial obligations, wondering how she would make ends meet each month. The excitement of owning her home sometimes overshadowed the growing concern about her ability to manage the mortgage payments, maintain a steady income and still save for the future.

Despite the significant strides she had made in other areas of her life, finances remained a point of stress for Jules. The $1,200 she once had in her bank account had grown, but not without a steep learning curve. There were moments of impulse spending, sometimes as a reward for her hard work, that later led to regret when she had to dip into her savings to cover unexpected expenses. She was still learning how to balance enjoying her life in the present with securing her financial future.

Jules' kids were now in their mid-teens. While it was not always smooth sailing as they found their way in life, testing boundaries and seeking independence, she had excellent relationships with them all. They were open and honest, and they had a deep, unconditional love for each other that could withstand any challenge.

Jules had also met a wonderful, kind, intelligent man online called Jeremy, who had a great sense of humour. They'd been dating for a few years, and he was a father to two adult kids. They talked about moving in together, although they were in no rush; perhaps when Jules' kids were a little older. They were content to spend time together when they could, thoroughly enjoying each other's company and looking forward to a European trip—a trip that, while exciting, also made Jules anxious about the cost and whether it would further strain her finances.

Jules' friendship group had evolved somewhat from the years before. She enjoyed attending Penny's annual retreat and made more like-minded friends who shared her holistic interests. While she still enjoyed catching up with her lifelong friends, it was nice to have different friendships to bring more harmony and moderation to her life.

Jules loved to start her day with meditation, journaling and practising gratitude. The gym, a walk, or a swim in the ocean would sometimes follow this. Now and again, she indulged in a few drinks at dinner with friends or at a party. But the days of drinking daily were long behind her, something for which she was so grateful.

However, Jules knew there was still more to learn and more to achieve. She had come so far, yet the lingering stress around finances served as a reminder that her journey towards complete financial freedom and empowerment wasn't over. This chapter is about Jules' continued growth—learning how to manage wealth wisely, make informed financial decisions, and build a future where she feels truly secure and free.

THIS CHAPTER HIGHLIGHTS the crucial role of financial wellbeing in living a worthy and wealthy life. It starts by encouraging you to become aware of your unique money mindset and addressing any negative beliefs limiting your financial success. By cultivating good money habits, you can empower yourself and enhance your security and freedom. You'll also find tips and tricks for improving your financial literacy so you can feel more confident in every decision you make for your future.

At this stage in your journey, it's essential to consider the role financial wellbeing plays in living a truly worthy and wealthy life. While money is merely a tool, it serves an undeniable purpose in providing safety and security, enabling you to care for yourself and those you are responsible for. While financial wealth may not directly equate to happiness, it certainly helps meet your basic needs. Having your basic needs met provides the foundation for an abundant life.

According to Maslow's hierarchy of needs, once your physiological requirements—such as food, water and shelter—are met, your focus can shift to fulfilling higher-level needs like love, belonging, self-esteem and, ultimately, self-actualisation. In the modern world, money plays a pivotal role in helping you achieve all of this. It ensures that you can provide the essentials for yourself and your loved ones, laying the groundwork for deeper fulfilment.

Yet, it's important to note that while money contributes to life satisfaction, its influence on emotional wellbeing only goes so far. Research by Nobel laureates Angus Deaton and Daniel Kahneman reveals that beyond a certain income level, financial wealth has a diminished impact on emotional wellbeing. Instead, factors such as meaningful relationships, personal growth and a sense of purpose take on greater significance in determining long-term happiness. In other words, true wealth extends far beyond your bank account.[7]

That said, financial stability remains a critical pillar in achieving overall wellbeing. It provides the freedom to pursue your goals, the security to weather life's challenges, and the empowerment to live on your own terms. Understanding your unique money mindset and developing financial empowerment are essential next steps towards creating lasting wealth in terms of material abundance and personal fulfilment.

Your Money Mindset

Your relationship with money is deeply rooted in your past, often shaped during your formative years by early experiences and the attitudes you observed from your primary caregivers. These influences, absorbed primarily during the

---

7   https://spia.princeton.edu/sites/default/files/content/docs/news/Happiness_Money_
Summary.pdf

imprint period, frequently become ingrained as your personal truth, consciously or unconsciously impacting how you handle finances as an adult.

In Chapter 1: Chrysalis, we explored how limiting beliefs shape your self-worth and relationships, and the same concept applies to money. Limiting beliefs about money, if left unchecked, can continue to influence your financial decisions, causing stress and holding you back from financial growth and empowerment. By uncovering these ingrained beliefs and reframing your approach, you can begin to reshape your relationship with money.

Here are some common limiting money mindsets that may be holding you back:

- **Scarcity mentality**: The belief that there is never enough. This often leads to fear-based decisions, such as hoarding money or being overly frugal to avoid financial insecurity. This mindset is tied to limiting beliefs such as 'money doesn't grow on trees' or 'you have to work hard to earn money'. The scarcity mindset mirrors emotional patterns where you might feel unworthy of abundance and continuously fear not having enough, both financially and emotionally.

- **Money is harmful**: Some people associate wealth with greed or corruption, subconsciously blocking opportunities to accumulate wealth because of negative connotations. This mindset is rooted in beliefs like 'money is the root of all evil' or 'having money makes me a bad person'. These limiting thoughts may cause you to subconsciously reject financial growth, sabotaging your ability to build wealth.

- **Passive financial approach**: This belief involves avoiding financial management or feeling that handling finances is someone else's responsibility. It is often tied to the idea of 'burying your head in the sand' and can stem from a lack of financial education, fear of making mistakes, or financial control by another person. Like low self-worth, avoiding financial decisions can be driven by feelings of inadequacy or fear of failure.

Each of these mindsets can limit your ability to build and sustain financial wellbeing. However, by creating awareness around them, you can begin to shift towards a more positive and empowered financial mindset.

Journal Prompt—Money Mindset

Use the following prompts to dive deeper into your relationship with money and begin identifying limiting beliefs that may be affecting you:

Step 1—Explore Money Beliefs Inherited from Primary Caregivers

- What beliefs about money did you learn from your mum, dad or primary caregivers? Reflect on the conversations you overheard about money. Were they positive or filled with stress and fear? This can provide insight into the beliefs you absorbed as a child.

- How did your caregivers earn, save and spend money? Think about their habits around money. Did they save diligently or spend freely? How did they handle debt? These habits often pass down from one generation to the next.

- Did your caregivers fight or calmly discuss finances? Reflect on the emotional environment surrounding money in your home. Was it a source of tension, or did your caregivers discuss it openly and without conflict?

- How did your caregivers talk about wealthy people? What attitudes did they express about people with wealth? Did they celebrate their success or criticise them for being greedy or unwholesome? This can shape how you feel about your own potential to accumulate wealth.

Step 2—Reflect on Your Financial Situation Growing Up

- Was there enough money growing up, or was it a struggle? Consider how your childhood experiences with money affected you. Did scarcity in your home make you anxious about spending, or did wealth make you complacent about managing your finances?

- What historical era did you grow up in? Where are you in your family's birth order (e.g., eldest, youngest)? Reflect on how economic conditions during your childhood or your family dynamics may have influenced your views on money.

- How did your family lifestyle affect your early view of success? Reflect on how your family's financial status shaped your perceptions of success and happiness. Did it create pressure, or did it provide a sense of comfort?

Step 3—Consider the Impact of Your Money Beliefs Today

- How do the beliefs you inherited affect your relationship with money today? Trace the connection between your childhood experiences and your current financial habits. For example, if your parents were overly frugal, do you now feel guilty about spending on yourself?

- What limiting beliefs do you notice in your financial decisions today? Explore how your beliefs may hold you back, like avoiding financial risks or feeling anxious when spending. Do you associate spending money with guilt or fear?

- Are there any positive money habits you've inherited? Not all inherited money beliefs are limiting. Reflect on positive financial habits or mindsets you've adopted that have served you well.

Step 4—Reframing Your Money Beliefs

- Which beliefs no longer serve your financial wellbeing? Consider how your current money beliefs are serving you. Are these beliefs still true for you? Reflect on which ones feel outdated, unhelpful, or no longer aligned with your reality, and which ones support your growth.

- How can you start shifting your mindset to create healthier financial habits? Write down any new beliefs you'd like to adopt about money. For example, 'I am worthy of financial abundance,' or 'I manage my money with confidence and clarity.'

By using these prompts to explore and reflect on your financial history, you're taking a crucial step towards building a healthier, more empowering relationship with money. Becoming aware of the money beliefs you've inherited allows you to reshape them and move forward with greater financial empowerment. For example, if you have a scarcity mindset, you might feel there is never enough money, no matter how much you actually have. As you address and reframe these beliefs, you'll regain control over your financial future and lay the foundation for lasting wealth and abundance.

Financial Empowerment

Once you gain clarity about your unique money mindset, the next step is to establish a financial budget. A budget helps you stay present and informed about your financial situation, offering a clearer picture of how you spend, save and invest.

Financial empowerment isn't solely about how much money you have; it's about how effectively you manage what you have. For example, someone who earns a lot may still struggle to manage their finances, overspending or accumulating debt, leaving them feeling financially insecure. Conversely, someone with a more modest income may live within their means, feeling in control and empowered by managing their finances well.

Creating a budget may take some time upfront, but once you gather the necessary data and set up automation for your bills and investments, you'll feel more confident, reduce your mental load and gain peace of mind. In the end, knowledge is power. The more you know about your financial situation, the more choices you'll have.

To help you get started, you can download my free Money Mindfulness Budget Planner from my website at www.emmal-agerlow.com/free-money-mindfulness-budget-planner.

Creating a Realistic Budget

A realistic budget reflects your needs and lifestyle. It allows for occasional indulgences but prioritises saving and investing for the future. Here's how to create one:

1   **Calculate your income**: Include all income sources, such as salary, business earnings, investment returns (e.g., interest or dividend payments), and government or benefit payments.

2   **Review past spending**: List every recurring bill, such as rent/mortgage, groceries, transportation and entertainment. Don't forget to allocate amounts for non-essential spending, such as dining out, subscriptions or impulse purchases.

3   **Choose the frequency for your plan**: Whether you prefer to budget monthly, weekly or fortnightly depends on your pay schedule and personal preference. Ensure all income and expenses are aligned with the same time frame.

4   **Make a plan**: Enter your data into a budgeting tool or download the free Money Mindfulness Budget Planner from my website.

5   **Adjust where necessary**: Review your expenses and identify areas where you can cut back if you're spending more than your income. Consider both small changes, like ordering groceries online and reducing takeaways, and larger ones, such as car loans or negotiating rental costs. Remember, a budget is a living document that evolves with your financial situation. It's important to allow some room for spontaneity and small indulgences while keeping your long-term goals in focus. This balance helps make budgeting more sustainable and enjoyable.

6   **Set realistic goals**: Set both short- and long-term financial goals. Short-term goals might include saving for a holiday or paying off existing debt, while long-term goals could involve saving for a home, paying off a mortgage, or planning for retirement.

7   **Review your budget regularly**: As the cost of living or your circumstances change, it's important to regularly review your plan. Consider a monthly check-in for minor adjustments and an annual review for a more in-depth assessment.

Budgeting success tip:
Remember, budgeting isn't about restriction—it's about gaining control and freedom over where your money goes so you can enjoy life without financial stress.

CLIENT STORY

One notable financial success story is Mel, a client who initially came to me for private coaching with the goal of bringing structure and clarity to her finances while maximising her wealth potential.

Through our sessions, Mel gained the accountability and support needed to refine her budgeting practices and cultivate a strong sense of money mindfulness—both essential components of developing a wealthy mindset. By becoming more intentional with her financial habits and strengthening her long-term wealth-building strategies, Mel transformed her relationship with money.

Today, Mel has gained her wings, reaping the rewards of her financial discipline. She feels empowered and financially secure, enabling her to live abroad and travel around Australia for extended periods with her family, all while trusting that her wealth-building strategy is working for her. By setting clear financial goals and focusing on strategic property investments, Mel has built a solid foundation for future wealth while still enjoying a rich and fulfilling life in the present.

Her story exemplifies the true strength of financial empowerment. Through intentional financial habits, budgeting, and a growth-oriented money mindset, Mel has aligned her wealth with her values, allowing her to achieve both immediate financial goals and long-term security. This journey highlights how true wealth goes beyond financial success to include fulfilment, purpose, meaningful connections and experiences, and time autonomy.

Breaking Negative Money Habits

Recognising and breaking negative money habits is key to achieving financial empowerment. While it's important to allow yourself occasional treats within your budget, frequent impulse spending, emotional purchases or failing to save consistently can hold you back. Start by identifying patterns of impulsive spending and the triggers behind them, whether emotional or situational.

Journal Prompt—Breaking Negative Money Habits

Set aside thirty minutes and use the following prompts to explore your spending habits and identify areas where you can improve:

Step 1—Review Your Spending

- Look back at your spending over the past month. How many purchases were impulse buys? What emotions or situations triggered these purchases? Awareness is the first step towards change.

Step 2—Reflect on the Impact

- How did you feel after making these purchases? Did they bring lasting satisfaction, or did you experience regret or guilt afterwards? Understanding the emotional drivers behind impulse spending can reveal areas where boundaries are needed.

Step 3—Set New Intentions

- What specific changes can you make to curb impulsive spending? It's not about cutting out indulgences completely but about creating intentional boundaries that allow for spontaneity without derailing your financial plan. Consider healthy changes like limiting online shopping at certain times, removing payment information from websites, or shifting your mindset from shopping as a reward to self-care activities that don't involve spending. For self-care ideas, revisit Chapter 3—Nectar.

Step 4—Create a Savings Plan

- Establish realistic savings goals and automate your savings. Even small contributions can build motivation, accountability and a financial buffer, helping you prevent the urge to spend impulsively. Reflect on how saving aligns with your long-term financial goals and overall wellbeing.

By journaling on these prompts, you'll begin to identify emotional spending triggers and build healthier financial habits. Understanding where and why you spend impulsively will empower you to make more intentional choices that support your financial wellbeing.

Building Wealth and Financial Literacy

Wealth is the accumulation of something desirable, and when it comes to finances, wealth is often measured by your net worth—the total sum of your savings, investments, and cash minus any debts (liabilities). In other words, financial wealth reflects having more assets than liabilities, often referred to as equity.

Building wealth starts with increasing your financial literacy, meaning building a confident understanding of key concepts like saving, investing and debt management. Financial literacy leads to a stronger sense of wellbeing and self-trust. Financial education, on the other hand, is the ability to understand how financial resources work and to make informed decisions.

Here are a few common strategies to grow your financial wealth:

- **Invest in property**: Real estate can build wealth through appreciation and rental income. Property values often rise over time, providing long-term financial stability.

- **Invest in shares and ETFs**: Shares or stocks represent ownership in a company, while exchange traded funds (ETFs) offer a diversified basket of shares, reducing risk. Both can grow wealth over time, though they carry varying levels of risk.

- **Low-risk investments**: For risk-averse individuals, options like savings accounts, bonds or term deposits provide security. These don't offer high returns but do offer stability.

- **Higher-risk investments**: Foreign exchange trading or cryptocurrencies like bitcoin may offer high returns but come with greater risk. Ensure it fits your strategy and risk tolerance.

- **Start a business**: Entrepreneurship allows for multiple income streams and building equity.

- **Further education and training**: Investing in your education can impact your ability to earn more over time.

Understanding Risk Tolerance

Once you have a budget in place and are ready to invest, it's essential to explore your risk tolerance. This refers to how much financial risk you are comfortable taking to grow your wealth. Your risk tolerance is unique to your financial situation, goals and personality.

For instance, younger investors may have a higher risk tolerance since they have more time to recover from market downturns. However, as you near retirement age, your risk tolerance may decrease, and you may prefer lower-risk investments to protect your wealth.

General financial tips:

- **Reduce high-interest debt**: Focus on paying off credit cards or personal loans with high interest rates to free up more income for saving and investing.

- **Automate your finances**: Set up automatic payments for bills and regular expenses, as well as recurring transfers to savings or investment accounts. Automating your finances reduces the mental load and enhances accountability.

- **Make big and small lifestyle adjustments**: Look at both small, everyday expenses (like reducing takeaways or subscription services) and bigger commitments (like re-evaluating car loans, trading in for a more affordable vehicle, or reassessing housing costs). These adjustments can collectively impact your ability to live within your means and build savings.

- **Diversify investments**: Spread your wealth across asset classes like property, shares and ETFs to mitigate risk.

- **Increase financial literacy and education**: Commit to continuous learning about personal finance. The more you understand, the better your financial decisions will be.

- **Boost earning potential**: Invest in yourself through education or certifications that can lead to higher earnings such as a trade or a university degree.

- **Reassess financial goals**: As your life evolves, regularly reassess your financial goals and adjust your strategy to ensure you stay on track. Consider working with a financial advisor, especially as you approach retirement. If you plan to retire at age sixty-five, you'll need to ensure you have the financial resources to support yourself for an additional ten to thirty years, depending on your circumstances and longevity.

Building a solid financial foundation is the key to unlocking greater freedom in other areas of life. When you're in control of your finances, you no longer have to spend energy worrying about making ends meet or feeling constrained by debt. Instead, you gain the ability to make choices that align with your values, invest in experiences that bring you joy, and dedicate more time to the things that truly matter. With financial stability comes the autonomy to design a life that prioritises wealth *and* wellbeing.

As you take charge of your financial empowerment, you'll realise that one of the greatest luxuries money can afford is time—the freedom to spend it on your terms. In the next section, we'll explore how time, just like money, is a valuable resource that can be managed intentionally to create more meaningful and fulfilling experiences, helping you live a life that honours your worth, your purpose and your wellbeing.

AS JULES GREW more secure within herself, she realised the importance of applying the same intention and diligence to her finances. She established a realistic budget, gaining clarity over her spending and savings. By managing her money with confidence and intention, she diligently tracked her expenses, prioritised savings, and set clear financial goals aligned with her long-term vision.

This newfound financial empowerment enabled her to make informed decisions, like planning and budgeting for her European trip, which eased her anxiety about costs. Jules also made extra contributions to her mortgage and set up automated monthly investments in an ETF. While modest, these investments steadily contributed to her financial free-dom and helped curb impulse purchases she would later regret.

Her relationship with money transformed from a source of stress into a tool for creating the life she desired. Jules experienced a sense of freedom and empowerment, know-ing she had a solid financial foundation. This shift not only improved her financial situation but also enriched her life, allowing her to focus more on her psychology studies, rela-tionships, and experiences that bring her joy. By embracing a wealth mindset, Jules truly gained her wings, soaring towards a future of abundance and fulfilment.

CHAPTER HIGHLIGHTS

- **Transforming your money mindset**: Your relationship with money often stems from beliefs formed in early childhood, influenced by caregivers and significant life experiences. These subconscious beliefs can shape your financial behaviours as an adult. Common limiting mindsets like scarcity mentality, viewing money as harmful or taking a passive approach can hinder financial growth. By recognising and challenging these beliefs, you can cultivate a more empowered mindset, leading to healthier financial decisions.

- **The importance of financial empowerment**: Financial empowerment is about more than accumulating wealth; it's about managing your money effectively. Creating a realistic budget is crucial, giving you clarity and control over your finances. Understanding where your money goes and aligning it with your goals reduces stress and creates a path to financial freedom. This chapter provides guidance on crafting a sustainable budget that supports your long-term wellbeing and security.

- **Breaking negative money habits**: Identifying and changing negative money habits is essential for financial empowerment. By recognising patterns of impulsive spending and understanding their triggers, you can set new intentions and develop healthier habits. This chapter helps you review past spending, reflect on its impact, and establish a savings plan aligned with your long-term goals.

- **Building wealth and financial literacy**: Building wealth starts with financial literacy, understanding key strategies like investing in property, shares and low-risk options while also knowing your risk tolerance.

- **True wealth:** True wealth is the alignment of financial empowerment, self-worth, purpose, personal wellbeing, financial stability
  and time freedom. When you harmonise your values, set intentional goals and manage your resources purposefully, you create
  a life that feels abundant on every level.

5

FLY

I AM FREE

*See yourself living in abundance
and you will attract it.*

RHONDA BYRNE
Australian writer and producer

AS WE JOURNEY through life, we often find ourselves caught up in a whirlwind of responsibilities, much like Jules. At the start of her transformation, Jules was floundering under the weight of it all—lacking clear direction and living on autopilot. Even with a newfound sense of purpose, she still juggled multiple roles: studying, working and raising her kids. While fulfilling, she sometimes felt overwhelmed and struggled to fit everything in. The missing piece of the puzzle wasn't just about managing finances or finding fulfilment in her career; it was about reclaiming her time and focusing on what truly mattered.

This chapter delves into the concept of time as a form of freedom. Like money, how we choose to spend our time directly impacts our sense of fulfilment and wealth. It's easy to get lost in the busyness of life, mistaking it for productivity or purpose. But, as Jules discovered, it's crucial to discern the difference between being busy and being meaningfully engaged. By learning to manage her time better, she could focus on the important things—her growth, relationships and personal wellbeing.

To help navigate this journey, we'll explore strategies for mastering time management, such as Covey's Time Management Matrix, and how setting clear, purposeful goals can help create a more harmonious and fulfilling life. By shifting our mindset around time, just as we have with money, and setting clear goals, we can begin to manifest a life of true wealth, where every moment becomes an investment in our purpose and joy.

Time is Freedom

Time, like money, is another crucial resource that determines how we achieve a truly worthy and wealthy life. As the saying goes, time is money. How you spend your time can directly impact both your financial wellbeing and your overall sense of fulfilment. However, it's important to recognise the difference between being busy and being productive.

In today's society, being constantly busy is often seen as a badge of honour and a mark of self-worth, but busyness doesn't always equate to living a life of purpose. Like your relationship with money, your relationship with time can either propel you towards or away from a truly fulfilled life.

Take Jules, for example. In Chapter 1, her days were filled with endless busyness and an overwhelming to-do list. She was floundering under the weight of it all. The busyness acted like a rudder, keeping her ship on course but steering her away from personal fulfilment.

How do you, like Jules, start to remove the noise around being busy, so you focus more on your purpose and bring personal fulfilment to your life?

This book emphasises the importance of meaningful activities such as fostering connections and nurturing your body and mind. These activities are crucial for a fulfilling and truly wealthy life but often get pushed aside for more seemingly urgent tasks. Being present can make a real difference in your life mentally and financially, as you will excel more in what you do. Let's look at how you can manage your time better with Covey's Time Management Matrix.[8]

Step 1—Covey's Time Management Matrix

- Covey's time management matrix is divided into four quadrants to help you prioritise your time (see Figure 3):

Urgent and Important (QUADRANT I)	Important, Not Urgent (QUADRANT II)
Crises Emergencies Deadlines Pressing problems	Relationship building Enriching experiences Nurturing body and mind Personal growth Goals
Urgent, Not Important (QUADRANT III)	Neither Urgent Nor Important (QUADRANT IV)
Phone calls Emails Meetings Popular activities	Binge-watching TV Scrolling social media Procrastination tasks Idle chitchat Busywork/trivia

FIGURE 3 Covey's Time Management Matrix

8 Covey, S. R. 1989. *The 7 Habits of Highly Effective People: Powerful Lessons in Personal Change.* Simon & Schuster.

1   **Urgent and important**: This quadrant includes emergencies and deadlines, such as your child breaking their arm at school or an imminent project deadline at work. These events require immediate attention and energy.

2   **Not urgent and important**: These are activities like fostering meaningful connections, having enriching experiences and nurturing your body and mind. They are important for long-term wellbeing and fulfilment but can often be neglected for more urgent tasks.

3   **Urgent but not important**: This quadrant consists of interruptions like phone calls, emails and other distractions. Because these activities demand your immediate attention, they often divert your focus from more meaningful activities. For instance, you might pause a deep conversation with your partner to answer a ringing phone or feel compelled to respond to a work-related email during family time. Although these interruptions seem urgent in the moment, they often lack real importance in the broader context of your life and can pull you away from activities that truly matter.

4   **Not urgent and not important**: Activities in this quadrant include binge-watching Netflix or scrolling through social media. While it's fine to relax and unwind, spending too much time here can detract from cultivating meaningful relationships, experiences, overall wellbeing, and working towards your purpose.

Step 2—Document Your Time
• If, after reading about the time management matrix, you realise you struggle to make time for important but non-urgent activities, try using the matrix to track where and how long you're spending your time in each quadrant. This

exercise will help shift your mindset towards greater intentionality. By documenting your time and completing the matrix, you'll be able to identify where adjustments are needed. It's in this quadrant that you truly create an abundant and fulfilled life beyond money, as you focus on nurturing your relationships, wellbeing and personal growth.

Step 3—Leverage Digital and Everyday Tools

* Other tools that can help you free up your time include planning and scheduling tasks in your phone calendar, setting timers for activities like cleaning, mindless scrolling on your phone or binge-watching Netflix, and removing unnecessary notifications. Utilising screen time settings on your phone and computer can also help. Additionally, try checking emails and apps only at specific times during the day. Delegation and outsourcing are other effective strategies to free up your time at work and home.

As you begin to apply these time management strategies, you'll notice that dedicating more time to important but non-urgent tasks brings greater fulfilment. These activities, like taking holidays, enjoying nights out with friends, or spending quality time with family, are the nectar that adds richness to life. This quadrant also includes the practices we discussed in Chapter 3, such as nurturing your wellbeing, engaging in self-care and fostering personal growth. While these activities may not demand immediate attention, they are essential for long-term health, happiness, abundance and fulfilment, acting as preventative measures that support a balanced and meaningful life.

We want to spend as much time as possible in this quadrant because it is here that we truly nurture our relationships, our joy and our sense of purpose. However, this can be challenging because time spent here is not urgent in nature, and it's easy to overlook or delay when something more urgent comes along like the ping of an email or the ring of a phone. Prioritising these non-urgent but important activities requires intentional effort, but the rewards are undeniable.

When you manage your time effectively and intentionally prioritise these experiences, you'll not only see the benefits in your productivity but also in the quality of your relationships and your overall wellbeing. You'll feel more in control of your life as you align your daily activities with your core values, your worth and your purpose.

Goal Setting

As you begin to master time management, you'll find more freedom to focus on activities that align with your values and purpose. But to truly maximise this newfound time and ensure you're moving towards your most fulfilling and abundant life, setting clear, actionable goals is essential.

But first, what are goals? Goals are dreams with deadlines. They help you clarify what you want and how to achieve it.

Journal Prompt—Visualisation

Visualise yourself living in full alignment with your purpose five years from now. What does your life look like? How do you spend each day? How do you feel physically, emotionally and spiritually?

Let this vision serve as a beacon, guiding each step you take towards a more purposeful life. You might even want to write a letter to your future self—describe everything in vivid detail. Where are you? What are you wearing? What does your environment look like? Allow yourself to dream fully, letting your hopes, dreams and deepest desires shape the narrative of your future self. Once you have a vision of what your best life looks like, start thinking about what steps you must take to achieve that dream.

SMART goals take this a step further. SMART stands for specific, measurable, achievable, relevant, and time-bound. By setting SMART goals, you can accurately assess and measure your progress, ensuring a clear plan that guides you and keeps you on track.

As you read this book, you might already have some ideas for goals you'd like to achieve; they can be financial or soulful wealth-building goals. Below are some examples that may inspire you:

- Develop healthy habits
- Break unhealthy habits
- Make time for self-care
- Lose weight
- Be fitter
- Start budgeting
- Improve your financial education and start investing
- Study
- Start a new career
- Change jobs
- Start a business
- Volunteer
- Improve relationships
- Rekindle or start a hobby or special interest
- Write a book
- Save for a holiday
- Buy a new home
- Move somewhere entirely new

Once you have a few goals in mind, it's important to check in to see if they align with your core values and overall purpose in life. Setting and achieving healthy goals is essential for fulfilment.

Goal setting helps you visualise what it is you want to achieve for your future and ensure that you are working towards a truly wealthy life. Another way to check whether your goals align is to consider the words you would like written about you on your tombstone or in your obituary when you pass away.

I know this may be a scary thought right now, but journaling on this can give you a greater perspective on your goals and life in general.

You can even convert it into a personal vision statement incorporating every area of your wealth, including self-worth, purpose, wellbeing, relationships and experiences, finances and time autonomy.

Doing this exercise can help uncover where you may have misplaced priorities if you place more importance on your financial wealth by prioritising your business or career over maintaining your wellbeing or relationships. Money and career success can often come at the cost of wellbeing and connection.

Bronnie Ware's book, *The Top Five Regrets of the Dying*, emphasises this idea with her widely quoted top five regrets of the dying, which include:

1 I wish I'd had the courage to live true to myself, not the life others expected of me.
2 I wish I hadn't worked so hard.
3 I wish I'd had the courage to express my feelings.
4 I wish I had stayed in touch with my friends.
5 I wish I had let myself be happier.

'I wish I hadn't worked so hard' is the regret I would like to bring to your attention and the premise for this book. Living a truly wealthy life goes beyond financial success and career achievements; it's about avoiding those end-of-life regrets. By knowing and living your purpose, finding the courage to express your true feelings, and making time for enriching relationships and experiences, you can create a life of happiness and fulfilment.

Take time with each step and be honest and specific in your responses. Ideally, set aside thirty to forty-five minutes. This exercise will provide a solid foundation for effectively setting and achieving your goals.

Goal Setting Exercise

Let's dive into clarifying your goals with this step-by-step exercise. Take the time to work through these prompts for at least three separate goals. This process will enhance your clarity and increase your chances of achieving them, ultimately fulfilling you.

Step 1—Set Your SMART Goal

• Define your goal using the SMART criteria. What specific actions will you take? When will you know you have accomplished your goal? Is it achievable? Does it align with your values and relate to your life and personal vision statement? Define a clear timeline for achieving your goal.

Step 2—Assess Urgency and Importance

• Consider whether your goal falls into the urgent or important category, as discussed in the Time Management Matrix earlier in this chapter.

Step 3—Evaluate Impact

* Reflect on whether this goal serves your wellbeing and/ or benefits others. Understanding the impact of your goal can increase your motivation to pursue it.

Step 4—Envision Your Future

* Journal about your future vision for each goal. Imagine what your life will look like once you've achieved your goal. Visualise yourself in the future, having accomplished what you set out to do.

Step 5—Identify Required Skills

* List the skills you will need to develop and hone to work towards and achieve your goal. Identifying these skills will help you create a skill acquisition and development plan.

Step 6—Identify Support and Resources

* Take inventory of the support and resources available to you. This could include people, tools, knowledge, or any other resources that can aid you in moving forward towards your goal. Acknowledging these resources will help you leverage them effectively on your journey.

CLIENT STORY

Simone, a private client and a successful career woman, came to me feeling like her busy life was on autopilot and her self-worth was at a low ebb after exiting a toxic romantic relationship. Despite having young children, Simone has an excellent growth mindset and was open to implementing self-care practices to support herself. At the beginning of our coaching relationship, I suggested Simone download the Insight Timer app and try meditating. After learning that she enjoyed writing, I encouraged her to journal and practise gratitude. Simone decided that the evening, after her young children were in bed, was best for these activities. At the end of our coaching tenure, we set a SMART goal for Simone to continue these activities indefinitely as she had experienced immeasurable benefits to her overall peace of mind by having them in place.

The SMART goal was to continue self-care practices (meditation, journaling and practising gratitude), generally daily, but not to worry if she missed a day here and there; she decided this was achievable and that it related to her life and core values that are love, growth and independence. The goal was to be consistent.

Simone marked this goal as not urgent but important and good for her as well as for others, as it would support her to achieve her primary, long-term goals of being more present, grounded, calm, patient, fulfilled and a better role model for her colleagues, loved ones and children.

Simone was encouraged to journal on the benefits of cultivating these practices in the long term and how they would be a good foundation for her other SMART goals, which included finishing career-related studies, buying an investment property and going on an overseas holiday.

We also listed her skills of being organised, authentic and adaptable, as well as her love of writing, which would support her goal. She also had extended family that she could call on occasionally to make time for these self-care practices.

Since working together, Simone has messaged me that she has been journaling, reading and meditating most evenings, and it's helping with her anxiety. She forgot how much she loved writing, and the Insight Timer app is awesome; the diversity of meditation and being able to choose the length of a session suited her, and that time just before sleep was the happiest and most fulfilling part of her day.

Imagine having this feeling every single day.

It's possible, and it will lead to fulfilment. Prioritising your overall wellbeing is crucial to feeling worthy, as outlined in Chapter 3. Setting this goal provided Simone with clear accountability for what was needed to achieve it. Practising these rituals also gave Simone the time and space to reflect on her life, be present with her feelings and envision her future. This allowed her to set other goals aligned with her values, ultimately putting her on the path to creating a truly wealthy life.

Manifesting

Manifesting is another powerful tool to help you visualise and work towards achieving your goals. Dr Joe Dispenza, a renowned author, speaker and researcher in neuroscience, epigenetics and quantum physics, explains that the mind's ability to visualise and emotionally experience an event can create the same neurochemical changes as if the event were actually happening. This principle is central to manifesting, suggesting that by mentally rehearsing desired outcomes, you can influence your brain and body to align with those outcomes, ultimately bringing them into existence.

I've been using manifestation to bring this book to life, and if you're reading it right now, then there might be something to this whole manifestation idea.

Manifestation Exercise

This exercise will guide you through visualising your goals further and using the power of manifestation to bring them into reality. Remember, as you focus on your desired outcome and connect emotionally with it, you're rewiring your brain and body to align with that future. Set aside some quiet time for this exercise, ideally around fifteen minutes.

Step 1—Set the Stage
- Find a quiet and comfortable space where you won't be disturbed. Sit or lie down in a relaxed position, close your eyes, and take a few deep breaths. Let go of any tension in your body and focus on your breath.

Step 2—Clarify Your Intention
- Bring one specific goal to mind. It can be a personal, professional, financial or spiritual goal, but make sure it is something that resonates deeply with your values and purpose. Once you have the goal in mind, state it clearly and affirmatively to yourself. For example: 'I am financially secure and abundant.' 'I am living a life of purpose and joy.' 'I am healthy, strong and thriving.'

Step 3—Visualise Your Future Self

- Begin to visualise yourself having already achieved this goal. Picture yourself in the situation where this goal is fully realised. What does your life look like? Who is with you? How do you feel emotionally, mentally and physically?

- For instance, if your goal is financial freedom, visualise your bank account with the amount of money that makes you feel secure. Imagine your lifestyle, the places you visit, the freedom and opportunities this financial security affords you.

Step 4—Engage All Your Senses

- To strengthen this visualisation, engage all your senses.

  - What do you see in this future vision?

  - What sounds are around you?

  - What does it feel like emotionally and physically to be in this moment?

  - What can you smell or taste in this scenario?

- The more sensory details you bring into your visualisation, the more your brain will believe that this reality is possible.

Step 5—Embrace the Emotions

- Allow yourself to feel the emotions of having already achieved your goal. Feel the joy, the relief, the pride, the gratitude. Fully immerse yourself in these emotions, allowing them to flood your body and mind. This step is essential because emotions are powerful signals that help align your brain and body with your vision.

Step 6—Let Go of the How

- While holding on to your vision, release the need to control how and when it will happen. Trust that the universe, or your subconscious mind, is working behind the scenes to bring this vision to life. Your role is to stay aligned with the feeling of already having achieved it.

Step 7—End with Gratitude

- End this exercise by expressing gratitude for this future that is already on its way to you. Trust in the process and in your ability to manifest your goals.

Optional reflection: After completing your exercise, take a few moments to journal about your experience. How did it feel to connect with your future self? What emotions or insights surfaced during the process? Capture your thoughts to help reinforce your vision and intention.

Guided Meditation—Meeting Your Future Self

Allow fifteen minutes for this meditation, which is designed to help you connect with your future self—the person you are becoming as you work towards your goals. As you go through the process, you'll envision your future self with all the wisdom, confidence and success that awaits you.

Step 1—Settle into Stillness

Find a quiet, comfortable space. Close your eyes and take a deep breath in, then slowly exhale. As you continue to breathe in and out, begin to relax every part of your body, starting with your head and moving down to your toes. Feel the weight of your body sinking into the floor or chair. This is your time to be fully present.

Step 2—Visualise a Path Forward

Imagine you are standing at the beginning of a path. This path represents the journey of your life. With each step forward, you are walking closer to your future self. The air around you is clear, the path smooth, and each step brings you closer to clarity and purpose.

Step 3—Meet Your Future Self

In the distance, you see your future self, standing confidently. As you approach, notice how they radiate peace and fulfilment. They smile warmly at you, welcoming you to this moment.

Consider now the goal you are working towards. Your future self has achieved this goal you are working towards today. Take in their appearance. How do they look? How do they carry themselves? Notice their energy, their health and their joy.

Step 4—Have a Conversation with Your Future Self

Your future self invites you to sit down beside them. As you sit, they begin to share with you all the wisdom and insights they've gathered over the years. Ask them:

- What habits and actions have helped you achieve your goals?

- What do I need to let go of to move forward?

- What values have guided you over the past years?

Listen carefully to their responses. Let their words resonate with you.

Step 5—Embrace the Future Vision

Now, imagine yourself stepping into their shoes. You are now the future self. Feel the confidence and fulfilment that comes from living your purpose and achieving your dreams.

Notice how your daily life looks from this perspective:

- What do your relationships feel like?
- What experiences are enriching your life?
- How do you feel about your health and wellbeing?

Allow your senses to guide you here. What do you hear in the future? What are you feeling? What can you see, hear, smell and taste? The more you engage your senses, the more vivid this experience becomes. Take a moment to savour this version of yourself.

Step 6—Gratitude for the Journey

As you prepare to leave, take a moment to thank your future self for their wisdom and guidance. Feel the gratitude welling up inside you for the journey you've been on, for the wisdom gained, and for the abundance and fulfilment you embody.

As you begin to walk side by side with your future self, feel the sense of ease and joy in knowing that you are connected. Each step forward brings you closer to your goals and dreams. Take a deep breath in, and with the next exhale, gently bring your awareness back to the present moment. Open your eyes when you are ready, feeling refreshed, inspired and aligned.

Optional reflection: After this meditation, take a moment to journal about what your future self told you. Capture any insights or feelings that came up during the process. Reflect on the guidance and how it aligns with your current goals and vision.

MANIFESTATION, LIKE GOAL setting, is not just about wishful thinking but about aligning your mind, body and emotions with the future you desire. When you pair clarity of intention with consistent action and the ability to visualise your future self, you lay the foundation for a life that reflects your deepest values and purpose.

As you journey towards the conclusion of this book, remember that true wealth is more than financial abundance. It is a sense of worth, joy and purpose that comes from living in alignment with your dreams and embracing each day with intention. By mastering your mindset, manifesting your goals and applying these practical exercises, you will create a life that looks and feels abundant.

Take a moment, ideally around thirty minutes, to reflect on how far you've come and the new insights you've gained about living a truly wealthy life. This prompt will help you synthesise your true wealth goals, combining your sense of worth, purpose, wellbeing and financial stability into a cohesive vision for your future.

Journal Prompt—Synthesising Your Wealth Goals

Step 1—Reflect on Your Worth
- In what areas of your life do you feel most worthy? How have these feelings of worthiness grown throughout this journey?

- Are there any limiting beliefs or insecurities still holding you back from fully embracing your worth? What steps can you take to release them?

Step 2—Clarify Your Purpose
- What has become clearer to you about your purpose through reading this book?

- How does your purpose align with your values and the goals you've set for your future? Are there any areas of misalignment that need attention?

- If someone were to write your story, what would you want them to highlight about the purpose that guides your life?

Step 3—Envision Your Wellbeing
- What new habits or practices have you implemented to support your mental, emotional and physical wellbeing?

- How do you want to continue nurturing your connections and relationships, and how can they contribute to a harmonious and fulfilling life?

Step 4—Assess Your Financial Empowerment
- How have your perspectives on financial wealth and security shifted? Do you feel more empowered to manage your finances and work towards financial freedom?

- What concrete steps will you take to ensure your financial goals align with your sense of worth, purpose and wellbeing?

- How will you make space in your life for enriching experiences, like holidays and quality time with loved ones?

Step 5—Create a Vision for Your Future
- Take a moment to imagine your ideal future. What does a truly wealthy life look like for you, where worth, purpose, wellbeing, financial stability and freedom intersect?

As you reflect on these prompts, remember that true wealth extends far beyond money. It encompasses your sense of worth, your purpose, your wellbeing, and the relationships and experiences that enrich your life. This book has guided you on a journey of self-discovery, financial empowerment and purposeful living, showing that a truly wealthy life is about harmonising your inner and outer worlds.

By clarifying your worth, aligning with your purpose, nurturing your wellbeing and cultivating financial empowerment, you are creating the foundation for a life of abundance. As you move forward, remember that this journey is ongoing—it's about continual growth and realignment. Use this moment to solidify the goals that will guide you towards the life you truly desire, and feel free to revisit this book whenever your circumstances change, or you feel called to reassess.

Ultimately, a life well lived is one where you feel worthy, act with purpose, foster your wellbeing and manage your resources with intention. Let this vision guide you as you work towards building the wealth that matters most—one that honours every facet of your life.

AFTER WORKING ON her financial plan and goals, Jules was incredibly excited about her future. Her life had become all about everything in moderation. With enough self-care, movement, nourishment, supportive and meaningful connection, short- and long-term goals, and ultimately bucket loads of worthiness, she knew she deserved every bit of the abundance coming her way.

She talked about buying into the private psychology practice once fully qualified and couldn't wait to be a practising psychologist herself. She had a budget that she closely adheres to, was slowly but surely paying off her apartment and was confident in her ability to build financial wealth, giving her the freedom to live the life of her dreams. Jules was making time for the family and friends that are good for her and creating meaningful memories and experiences with them.

Jules had created a truly wealthy life for herself by focusing on each of the pillars—worth, purpose, wellness, wealth and freedom.

What a vast improvement from the Jules we met in Chapter 1.

WHILE YOU MAY not have the same aspirations as Jules or myself, I hope our stories have shown you what is possible. I hope it's also helped you to learn that financial wealth is important, but that is not what this book is all about.

Money is simply a means to your freedom, which we must ensure is accounted for in the overall scheme. Ultimately, true wealth is beyond financial wealth and incorporates worthiness, wellbeing, meaningful relationships and experiences, a sense of purpose, financial stability and time freedom. When you understand all that, you can be a wonderful role model for everyone around you, tread lightly on the planet, and create a sustainable and fulfilling life.

Remember, the journey to true wealth and fulfilment is a continuous process of self-discovery, goal setting and mindful action. By integrating the principles and tools discussed in this chapter, you can overcome obstacles and align your actions with your deepest values.

Embrace this journey with patience and persistence, and you will live a life rich in meaning, connection and joy.

CHAPTER HIGHLIGHTS

- **Time is a form of wealth**: Just like money, time is a valuable resource that can either be spent wisely or wasted. True time freedom comes when you prioritise meaningful activities, nurture wellbeing and relationships, and create space for experiences that enrich your life rather than living on autopilot and staying busy for the sake of it.

- **Setting goals to achieve a truly wealthy life**: Setting clear, actionable goals is essential for creating a life of purpose and abundance. SMART goals—specific, measurable, achievable, relevant and time-bound—help you stay focused and on track towards achieving your dreams.

- **Manifestation is a tool for realising your dreams**: Manifesting is the process of aligning your thoughts, emotions and actions with your vision for the future. By visualising your goals and embracing the emotions of having already achieved them, you bring yourself one step closer to turning your dreams into reality.

CONCLUSION

BUTTERFLY

Most people spend their lives attempting to be somebody they aren't, but the real power comes from accepting the truth of who you are and running with it to the very best of your ability.

KAIN RAMSAY
Founder of The Academy of
Modern Applied Psychology

JULES LEANS BACK in her armchair at her clinic and sighs contentedly, looking over her notes for the next client. She has been a practising clinical psychologist for two years now and finds deep fulfilment in every aspect of her career.

Now a partner in the psychology practice she has called home for the past ten years, Jules is surrounded by wonderful, supportive colleagues. The sun shines through the bay window and catches the diamond on her finger. She smiles, a rush of warmth flooding through her. Jeremy proposed six months ago, and together, they are happily planning their wedding. Chloe and Mia will be bridesmaids, while Jimmy and Jeremy's two sons will stand as groomsmen.

Her children, now young adults, still live at home but lead independent lives. Jules cherishes her close relationships with them and feels proud that they've thrived alongside her own personal growth.

In mind, body and spirit, Jules prioritises her wellbeing. She feels worthy in every sense of the word, her self-worth is unwavering, and her financial worth is healthy and abundant.

Reflecting on her journey, Jules is filled with gratitude. Her dear friend Penny, who introduced her to personal development at the retreat, and Amanda, her life coach, were instrumental in guiding her inward. Yet, ultimately, she is proud of herself for having the bravery to unearth who she truly is and what she truly wants, and for finding the courage to pursue it all.

Her life now is richer than she ever imagined possible.

WELCOME, BUTTERFLY!

You've journeyed all the way from Chapter 1: Chrysalis, completing exercises and journal prompts, reflecting deeply on who you are and identifying areas where your life may be out of harmony. Uncovering your core values and challenging the limiting beliefs that once held you back, you've diminished their power over you.

With a newfound understanding of the benefits of self-care, you're prioritising your wellbeing more than ever. By carving out time for yourself, you've become calmer, and more grounded, patient, present and self-aware. Unhealthy coping habits are being replaced by healthier choices that support your growth.

Your relationships have transformed as well. You might have let go of connections that no longer serve you and embraced those that enrich your life. Whether through self-care, travel, or being present with loved ones, you seek and enjoy meaningful experiences.

You've also clarified what you truly want in life. Your purpose, aligned with your values, guides you. You've set goals and are actively visualising and manifesting the life of your dreams.

Your dreams extend beyond material gains like winning the lottery, getting a promotion or amassing financial wealth, although financial stability remains an important pillar, as we explored in Chapter 4. You've realised that true wealth encompasses making time for all the pillars in your life and ensuring they are in harmony.

Like Jules, you now have the tools and insights to create a truly wealthy life rich in meaning, fulfilment and joy. Celebrate each step forward, no matter how small, and continue setting meaningful goals that guide you towards your best life.

This journey is ongoing. Continue to reflect on your growth, revisit the exercises, and allow your dreams to evolve as you do. And remember, I'm here to support you if you're ready to dive deeper or need personalised guidance. Together, we can continue this journey of self-discovery and growth, ensuring that you live a life that is not just financially abundant but also profoundly fulfilling.

Thank you for allowing me to be part of your journey. Here's to a future where you feel truly worthy and wealthy in all areas of your life.

ACKNOWLEDGEMENTS

THIS BOOK HAS been a lifetime in the making and would certainly not have been possible without my tribe, who have supported and lifted me throughout my life.

Firstly, I would like to thank my husband, Aaron. You have always been there for me through my crazy ideas and the many iterations of Emma over the past thirty-odd years that we have known each other. I appreciate you supporting me as I grew my entrepreneurial wings and locked myself away to write this book.

Thanks also to my four kids—Ben, Ella, Zoe and Sarah—for giving me the grace and space to write. I hope that watching me go after my dreams has inspired you. Being your role model is my greatest achievement.

A heartfelt thanks to my extended family members who have championed me as I have put myself out there. Your encouragement has been invaluable.

To my friends, thank you for coming on this journey with me. A special shoutout to those I reached out to and who became characters in the book—Todd and Laura Tarlington, Cathy Roberts, Rachel and Justine, among others. My apologies for being unceremoniously cut to make room for my readers to be the heroes.

My deepest gratitude to all my beta readers. Your responses, endorsements and testimonials of *Worthy and Wealthy* mean the absolute world to me.

To Avril Lillian, a highly valued member of my team—I appreciate you more than you know. I credit your design genius and business acumen for giving me the confidence to take the leap of faith and start my business.

To all the new connections since embarking on my entrepreneurial path, you have enriched my life endlessly. To all the authors and guests I have met and interviewed on my podcast, *It's a Mindset*, thank you for your inspiration.

Special thanks to Kelly Irving, the entire Expert Author Community, Laetitia Andrac, my business doula, and Bernard Kates for their guidance and inspiration.

A special mention to Olivia Joerges, my editor, and Julia Kuris, my book designer, along with the team at Grammar Factory. Your expertise made the process of publishing this book a seamless and enriching experience.

To my clients and community, especially those cherished clients who allowed me to write about them in my book—thank you for trusting me.

Lastly, to you, my dear readers—thank you for picking up this book and reading until now. My deepest hope is that it provides you with a roadmap to live your most abundant and fulfilling life. I'd love for you to send me a DM on Instagram @emmalagerlow and share your 'aha' moments.

Ultimately, know that you are worthy and deserving of all the wealth in the world. Thank you for reading.

RESOURCES

'VE CREATED a Worthy and Wealthy PDF Journal Work-
book to support your journey, featuring all the journaling
exercises from the book.

Download your free copy at:
www.emmalagerlow.com/worthy-wealthy-workbook

You'll also find additional tools mentioned in the book, like
the 7-Day Self-Care Challenge and the Money Mindfulness
Budget Planner, in the Free Resources section on my website.

Explore more at: www.emmalagerlow.com

Keep growing and embracing your path to true abundance
and fulfilment.

ABOUT
THE AUTHOR

MMA LAGERLOW is a multi-passionate entrepreneur dedicated to helping individuals unlock true wealth in every aspect of life. As a mother of four teens, wife, daughter, sister and friend, Emma embraces the complexities of modern life while leading with purpose and authenticity.

With over twenty-five years of experience across sales, marketing, banking, finance and the pharmaceutical industry, Emma has honed her expertise in wealth creation and management. She has worked with industry giants like JPMorgan, Standard Chartered Bank and UBS, and holds a Bachelor of Business degree in Marketing, as well as a life coaching certification from Achology, The Academy of Modern Applied Psychology. This diverse background forms the foundation of Emma's approach as a holistic wealth and mindset coach, where she combines financial acumen with personal growth strategies to guide clients towards financial freedom, holistic wellbeing and purpose-driven living.

Emma has supported hundreds of clients through masterclasses, private coaching and corporate workshops, helping individuals and teams achieve meaningful transformations. Her unique blend of financial insight and a deep commitment to personal development creates a comprehensive pathway for clients to achieve lasting wealth and fulfilment.

Emma is also the host of the *It's a Mindset* podcast where she shares transformative insights and interviews, inspiring guests who offer personal growth wisdom and perspectives on true wealth. Her book, *Worthy and Wealthy*, is a testament to her mission to help readers cultivate a mindset that attracts abundance and nurtures self-worth.

In addition to her coaching and podcasting, Emma is a proud Community Host at The Expert Author Community, supporting aspiring authors on their writing journeys. She also volunteers as a meditation leader for Meditation HQ, hosting in-person meditation and sound healing events to encourage deeper self-care and wellbeing.

If you're ready to transform your mindset, improve your relationship with money and experience true fulfilment, Emma Lagerlow is here to support you. Explore her free resources and self-paced coaching programs, or dive deeper into transformation with her *Become the Butterfly* three-month one-on-one coaching experience, where she will personally guide you towards lasting, meaningful change. Together, you'll create a roadmap towards financial freedom, abundance and a deeply fulfilling life.

Connect with Emma on her website emmalagerlow.com, on Instagram @emmalagerlow, or listen to her podcast *It's a Mindset* on major podcast platforms.